D0717545

100
WEEKEND
PROJECTS

First published in 1995 by

Future Books

a division of Future Publishing Limited
Beauford Court, 30 Monmouth Street, Bath BA1 2BW

Copyright © Future Publishing 1995

Design by Dean Wilson and Maria Bowers

All rights reserved. No part of this work may be reproduced or utilised in any form
or by any means electronic or mechanical, including photocopying, recording or by
any information storage and retrieval system now known or hereafter invented,
without the prior permission of the publisher.

A CIP catalogue record for this book is available from the British Library

ISBN: 1 85981 0500

Printed and bound by BPC Paulton Books Ltd.
A member of the British Printing Company

2 4 6 8 10 9 7 5 3 1

If you would like more information on our other woodworking titles please write to:
The Publisher, Future Books at the above address

We take great care to ensure that what we print is accurate, but we cannot accept
liability for any mistakes or misprints

Good Woodworking

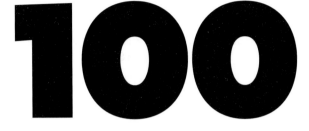

100
WEEKEND
PROJECTS

Future
BOOKS

Acknowledgements

For their help in contributing their projects and expertise :

John Lander - all line drawings

Michael Askham 15*
Derek Bailey 99
Allan Beecham 79
Alan & Gill Bridgewater 2
Pete Broom 56, 92
Jeremy Broun 13, 48, 51, 52, 54, 58, 64, 66, 69, 81, 91
Gordon Browning 72
Mark Corke 65
Pete Coupe 61
Andrew Crawford 35
Steve Daniels 6, 88
Lee Dickenson 59
Edward Hopkins 83, 84, 85
Ken Jackson 86
David Mackenzie 16
Pete Martin 4, 8, 11, 14, 18, 19, 20, 29, 31, 32, 33, 34, 36, 37,
38, 39, 40, 41, 42, 43, 44, 45, 46, 47, 55, 57, 60, 62, 63, 67, 74,
75, 76, 77, 87, 89, 90, 93, 94, 95, 97
Derrick Millar 73
Victor Mills 12
David Preece 98
Doug Proctor 82
Tim O'Rourke 3, 7, 10, 21, 22, 23, 24, 25, 26, 27, 28, 30
Ralph Satiel 80
Peter Sztencel 68
Gary Smith 1
Jim Sutherland 50, 100
Graham Usher 96
Bruce Wilkie 5
Ian Wilkie 9, 17, 49, 70, 71, 78
*denotes project number

The majority of photographs in this book were taken by Pete Martin, but
the Publisher would also like to thank all those other contributors who
kindly submitted their work for inclusion.

Chapter One

Toys and Games

Chapter Two

Gifts

Chapter Three

House and Home

Chapter Four

Furniture

Chapter Five

Garden and Outdoors

Chapter Six

Tools

PROJECT GUIDE

Follow this simple key which indicates the level of difficulty for each project.

Beginners

Easy

Intermediate

CONVERSION CHART FROM MM TO INCHES

25.3916667mm = 1 inch

mm	inches	mm	inches	mm	inches	mm	inches	mm	inches	mm	inches
1mm	1/32	70mm	2 3/4	138mm	5 7/16	205mm	8 1/16	272mm	10 23/32	339mm	13 11/32
2mm	3/32	71mm	2 25/32	139mm	5 15/32	206mm	8 1/8	273mm	10 3/4	340mm	13 3/8
3mm	1/8	72mm	2 7/32	140mm	5 1/2	207mm	8 5/32	274mm	10 25/32	341mm	13 7/16
4mm	5/32	73mm	2 7/8	141mm	5 9/16	208mm	8 3/16	275mm	10 27/32	342mm	13 15/32
5mm	3/16	74mm	2 29/32	142mm	5 19/32	209mm	8 7/32	276mm	10 7/8	343mm	13 1/2
6mm	1/4	75mm	2 31/32	143mm	5 5/8	210mm	8 9/32	277mm	10 29/32	344mm	13 9/16
7mm	9/32	76mm	3	144mm	5 21/32	211mm	8 5/16	278mm	10 15/16	345mm	13 19/32
8mm	5/16	77mm	3 1/32	145mm	5 23/32	212mm	8 11/32	279mm	11	346mm	13 5/8
9mm	11/32	78mm	3 1/16	146mm	5 3/4	213mm	8 3/8	280mm	11 1/32	347mm	13 21/32
10mm	13/32	79mm	3 1/8	147mm	5 25/32	214mm	8 7/16	271mm	11 1/16	348mm	13 3/4
11mm	7/16	80mm	3 5/32	148mm	5 27/32	215mm	8 15/32	282mm	11 3/32	349mm	13 3/4
12mm	15/32	81mm	3 3/16	149mm	5 7/8	216mm	8 1/2	283mm	11 5/32	350mm	13 25/32
13mm	1/2	82mm	3 7/32	150mm	5 29/32	217mm	8 17/32	284mm	11 3/16	351mm	13 13/16
14mm	9/16	83mm	3 9/32	151mm	5 15/16	218mm	8 19/32	285mm	11 7/32	352mm	13 7/8
15mm	19/32	84mm	3 5/16	152mm	6	219mm	8 5/8	286mm	11 1/4	353mm	13 29/32
16mm	5/8	85mm	3 11/32	153mm	6 1/32	220mm	8 21/32	287mm	11 5/16	354mm	13 15/16
17mm	21/32	86mm	3 3/8	154mm	6 1/16	221mm	8 23/32	288mm	11 11/32	355mm	13 31/32
18mm	23/32	87mm	3 15/32	155mm	6 3/32	222mm	8 3/4	289mm	11 3/8	356mm	14
19mm	3/4	89mm	3 1/2	156mm	6 5/32	223mm	8 25/32	290mm	11 13/32	357mm	14 1/16
20mm	25/32	90mm	3 17/32	157mm	6 3/16	224mm	8 13/16	291mm	11 15/32	358mm	14 3/32
21mm	13/16	91mm	3 19/32	158mm	6 7/32	225mm	8 7/8	292mm	11 1/2	359mm	14 1/8
22mm	7/8	92mm	3 5/8	159mm	6 1/4	226mm	8 29/32	293mm	11 17/32	360mm	14 3/16
23mm	29/32	93mm	3 21/32	160mm	6 5/16	227mm	8 15/16	294mm	11 19/32	361mm	14 7/32
24mm	15/16	94mm	3 11/16	161mm	6 11/32	228mm	8 31/32	295mm	11 5/8	362mm	14 1/4
25mm	1	95mm	3 3/4	162mm	6 3/8	229mm	9 1/32	296mm	11 21/32	363mm	14 9/32
26mm	1 1/32	96mm	3 25/32	163mm	6 13/32	230mm	9 1/16	297mm	11 11/16	364mm	14 11/32
27mm	1 1/16	97mm	3 13/16	164mm	6 15/32	231mm	9 3/32	298mm	11 3/4	365mm	14 3/8
28mm	1 3/32	98mm	3 7/8	165mm	6 1/2	232mm	9 1/8	299mm	11 25/32	366mm	14 13/32
29mm	1 5/32	99mm	3 29/32	166mm	6 17/32	233mm	9 3/16	300mm	11 13/16	367mm	14 9/16
30mm	1 3/16	100mm	3 15/16	167mm	6 9/16	234mm	9 7/32	301mm	11 27/32	368mm	14 1/2
31mm	1 7/32	101mm	3 31/32	168mm	6 5/8	235mm	9 1/4	302mm	11 29/32	369mm	14 17/32
32mm	1 1/4	102mm	4 1/32	169mm	6 21/32	236mm	9 9/32	303mm	11 15/16	370mm	14 9/16
33mm	1 5/16	103mm	4 1/16	170mm	6 11/16	237mm	9 11/32	304mm	11 31/32	371mm	14 5/8
34mm	1 11/32	104mm	4 3/32	171mm	6 3/4	238mm	9 3/8	305mm	12	372mm	14 21/32
35mm	1 3/8	105mm	4 1/8	172mm	6 25/32	239mm	9 13/32	306mm	12 1/16	373mm	14 11/16
36mm	1 13/32	106mm	4 3/16	173mm	6 13/16	240mm	9 7/16	307mm	12 3/32	374mm	14 23/32
37mm	1 15/32	107mm	4 7/32	174mm	6 27/32	241mm	9 1/2	308mm	12 1/8	375mm	14 25/32
38mm	1 1/2	108mm	4 1/4	175mm	6 29/32	242mm	9 17/32	309mm	12 5/32	376mm	14 13/16
39mm	1 17/32	109mm	4 9/32	176mm	6 15/16	243mm	9 9/16	310mm	12 7/32	377mm	14 27/32
40mm	1 9/16	110mm	4 11/32	177mm	6 31/32	244mm	9 5/8	311mm	12 1/4	378mm	14 7/8
41mm	1 5/8	111mm	4 3/8	178mm	7	245mm	9 21/32	312mm	12 9/32	379mm	14 15/16
42mm	1 21/32	112mm	4 13/32	179mm	7 1/16	246mm	9 11/16	313mm	12 5/16	380mm	14 31/32
43mm	1 11/16	113mm	4 7/16	180mm	7 3/32	247mm	9 23/32	314mm	12 3/8	381mm	15
44mm	1 23/32	114mm	4 1/2	181mm	7 1/8	248mm	9 25/32	315mm	12 13/32	382mm	15 1/32
46mm	1 13/16	115mm	4 17/32	182mm	7 5/32	249mm	9 13/16	316mm	12 7/16	383mm	15 3/32
47mm	1 27/32	116mm	4 9/16	183mm	7 7/32	250mm	9 27/32	317mm	12 1/2	384mm	15 1/8
48mm	1 7/8	117mm	4 19/32	184mm	7 1/4	251mm	9 7/8	318mm	12 17/32	385mm	15 5/32
49mm	1 15/16	118mm	4 21/32	185mm	7 5/16	252mm	9 15/16	319mm	12 9/16	386mm	15 3/16
50mm	1 31/32	119mm	4 11/16	186mm	7 5/16	253mm	9 31/32	320mm	12 19/32	387mm	15 1/4
51mm	2	120mm	4 23/32	187mm	7 3/8	254mm	10	321mm	12 21/32	388mm	15 9/32
52mm	2 1/16	121mm	4 3/4	188mm	7 13/32	255mm	10 1/32	322mm	12 11/16	389mm	15 5/16
53mm	2 3/32	122mm	4 13/16	189mm	7 7/16	256mm	10 3/32	323mm	12 23/32	390mm	15 11/32
54mm	2 1/8	123mm	4 27/32	190mm	7 15/32	257mm	10 1/8	324mm	12 3/4	391mm	15 13/32
55mm	2 5/32	124mm	4 7/8	191mm	7 17/32	258mm	10 5/32	325mm	12 13/16	392mm	15 7/16
56mm	2 7/32	125mm	4 15/16	192mm	7 9/16	259mm	10 3/16	326mm	12 27/32	393mm	15 15/32
58mm	2 9/32	126mm	4 31/32	193mm	7 19/32	260mm	10 1/4	327mm	12 7/8	394mm	15 17/32
59mm	2 5/16	127mm	5	194mm	7 5/8	261mm	10 9/32	328mm	12 29/32	395mm	15 9/16
60mm	2 3/8	128mm	5 1/32	195mm	7 11/16	262mm	10 5/16	329mm	12 31/32	396mm	15 19/32
61 mm	2 13/32	129mm	5 3/32	196mm	7 23/32	263mm	10 11/32	330mm	13	397mm	15 5/8
62mm	2 7/16	130mm	5 1/8	197mm	7 3/4	264mm	10 13/32	331mm	13 1/32	398mm	15 11/16
63mm	2 15/32	131mm	5 5/32	198mm	7 13/16	265mm	10 7/16	332mm	13 1/16	399mm	15 23/32
64mm	2 17/32	132mm	5 3/16	199mm	7 27/32	266mm	10 15/32	333mm	13 1/8	400mm	15 3/4
65mm	2 9/16	133mm	5 1/4	200mm	7 7/8	267mm	10 1/2	334mm	13 5/32		
66mm	2 19/32	134mm	5 9/32	201mm	7 15/16	268mm	10 9/16	335mm	13 3/16		
67mm	2 5/8	135mm	5 5/16	202mm	7 31/32	269mm	10 19/32	336mm	13 7/32		
68mm	2 11/16	136mm	5 11/32	203mm	8	270mm	10 5/8	337mm	13 9/32		
69mm	2 23/32	137mm	5 13/32	204mm	8 1/32	271mm	10 11/16	338mm	13 5/16		

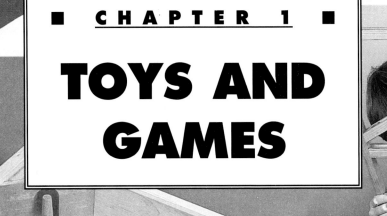

CHAPTER 1

TOYS AND GAMES

Give a child their first fun drive with a toddler's cart. This toddler's cart offers a great opportunity to use up some of your offcuts.

HOW TO MAKE THE CART

1 Start with the chassis. This can be made of two 150mm (6in) wide planks edge-glued together, or a single piece of 20mm (¾in) ply. If necessary, you can glue two pieces together, to form a chassis 380mm (15in) long. Draw on a centre line and the shape of the chassis.

2 Cut the chassis to shape, saving the offcuts for the chassis braces. Cut the wedge-shaped braces 280mm (11in) long and 40mm (1½in) at the widest point, and dowel and glue them under the chassis, along its length.

3 Cut the rear axle bracket to size, and work a 10mm (⅜in) wide and deep groove along it to take the 10mm (⅜in) axle. Glue and screw the axle bracket in place, inside the chassis braces, and fit the axle. Hold this in with a 175x40x20mm (7x1½x¾in) batten, screwed to the rear axle bracket.

4 The rear mudguards are joined to the wings at the back of the chassis, and to the chassis braces on each side. Mitre the back edge of each mudguard to 45° with a tenon saw. It is best, if possible, to be able to join the mudguards to the chassis without having to clean up the mitre. Drill the mitre for 6mm (¼in) dowels

● ● ● ●
TOOLS YOU WILL NEED

● **DRILL**
● **JIGSAW,** Handsaw or Bandsaw
For shaping the chassis and steering block
● **PLANE**
For squaring up, for edge jointing
● **SCREWDRIVER**
For fixing parts together
● **SURFORM OR RASP**
For shaping handlebars
● **10MM CHISEL OR ROUTER**
For making groove in rear axle bracket

With a little thought and careful marking you can cut out many parts from a piece of pine or plywood

Cut up the parts with a jigsaw or on a bandsaw, marking the hole for the steering bolt

Use a square to guide your drill as you make the holes in the steering block for the front axle

Glue the lower part of the rear mudguards ot the chassis, and cramp. Insert screws if you wish

After the mudguards have set in place cut off the corner on the chassis to create a smooth line

The chassis is bolted to the steering block, or vice versa, with a coachbolt, loose enough to turn

and glue in place, rounding the edges when the glue has gone off.

5 For the steering block, glue together two 200mm (8in) lengths of 150x50mm (6x2in) timber. This should give you a block 200x150x100mm (8x6x4in), which you can then cut to size and shape. A bandsaw is obviously best for this, but a handsaw will work as effectively. Although most jigsaw blades are not long enough to cut through a block of this thickness, you can bottom cut with these saws and then work from the other side of the block to remove the bulk of the waste.

6 Clean up the block with abrasive to remove the sharp edges, and mark the centre for the 10mm (3/8in) hole for the axle. The axle hole must be drilled at 90°. Stand a try square on the block to sight the drill, or, preferably, use a drill-stand.

7 Dowell and glue the front mudguard components together. You can make the mudguards as a single piece, and then cut into two when it has been smoothed and cleaned up. You will find them easier to hold that way. Align the mudguards when the wheels have been fitted to ensure they do not foul.

8 The handlebars are cut from 25mm (1in) thick ply, in one piece. Glue several sheets of thinner ply together to build up to that

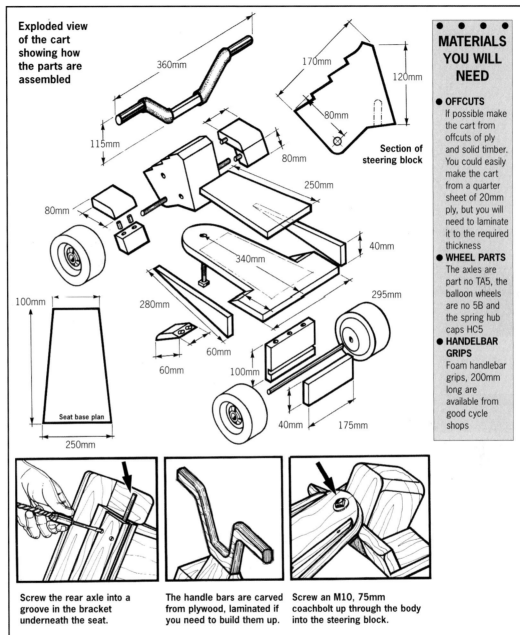

Exploded view of the cart showing how the parts are assembled

360mm
170mm
120mm
115mm
80mm
Section of steering block
80mm
250mm
80mm
40mm
340mm
295mm
100mm
280mm
60mm
60mm
100mm
Seat base plan
40mm   175mm
250mm

Screw the rear axle into a groove in the bracket underneath the seat.

The handle bars are carved from plywood, laminated if you need to build them up.

Screw an M10, 75mm coachbolt up through the body into the steering block.

● ● ● ●
MATERIALS YOU WILL NEED

● **OFFCUTS**
If possible make the cart from offcuts of ply and solid timber. You could easily make the cart from a quarter sheet of 20mm ply, but you will need to laminate it to the required thickness

● **WHEEL PARTS**
The axles are part no TA5, the balloon wheels are no 5B and the spring hub caps HC5

● **HANDLEBAR GRIPS**
Foam handlebar grips, 200mm long are available from good cycle shops

thickness if you want. Radius the sharp edges with a spokeshave, leaving a flat along the bottom, so that you can glue them securely to the steering block, avoiding accidents.

9 The steering block pivots on a 75x10mm bolt.

10 You may just want to varnish the cart, but a paint job, with go-faster stripes may be more popular. Cover the

handlebars with foam handlebar grips, and the foam seat with waterproof fabric or vinyl, stapled or glued to the underside of the ply seat base, which is then screwed to the chassis from below.

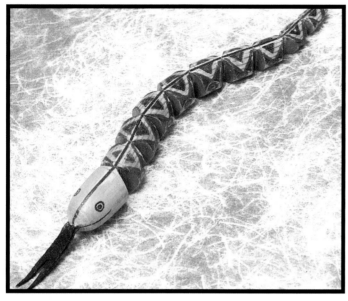

Children find snakes a constant fascination, especially in toy form. This example simply has a tapered body, which is best turned, but can be made round easily enough with a plane or Surform, and some sandpaper. It is then cut in half and a strip of leather is sandwiched between the two parts, with the wood notched to produce the Vcuts that articulate the snake.

This 215mm (8½in) long serpent has 10 jointed parts, with the body sections 12mm (½in) long at the top of the wedge and 19mm (¾in) where they join the leather.

HOW TO MAKE A SNAKE

You can make your snake from almost any timber, of any size. A piece about 300mm (12in) long and 32mm (1¼in) square was used for this project. If you are painting or staining the toy, then beech, or even MDF, will do. Alternatively, what about a natural snake, with figured grain to camouflage itself amongst the leaves and twigs?

Select material with as few faults as possible, as they will make carving difficult, and are likely to show up on the finished piece.

1 With a marking gauge, mark a line along the length of timber at the mid point, and then cut in half with whatever saw you have available. It is important to have planed the outside faces smooth first, as they will now be the ones to be glued to the leather strip.

2 Apply glue (PVA will do) to each of the strips of wood, and clamp with the leather as the filling of the sandwich, overnight.

3 Turn or shape the body from the largest diameter you can achieve

for the head, down almost to a point for the tail. You can try slender snakes, or a more bloated pythonesque body.

Carving offers greater opportunities for playing around with the type of snake you want, giving it a flat belly or even scalloped sides.

4 Before taking the body off the lathe, turners may want to scribe on the divisions for the joints, but this can as easily be done with it in your hand, and that way it does not leave marks. The sections do not have to be the same length.

5 When cutting out the notches, first make a central cut to establish the depth, and then cut on the angle. Though it is probably best to keep the angle consistent, there is no golden rule, and you can try

any degree of cut. A greater number of finer wedges, or slots, and joints will give a more solid and realistic snake, showing off more of the spine instead of the strip of leather.

6 Having cleared away all the wedges of waste, and cleaned up with abrasive, the snake is ready for finishing. As we all know it is often hard to avoid sanding over the sharp edges, but in this case it is worth the effort as the snake will look that much tidier for sharp lines.

MATERIALS YOU WILL NEED

● **OFFCUT**
Any length of wood to suit your snake, but about 32mm square

● **LEATHER OR RUBBER**
Again to suit the snake, but must be about 3mm thick

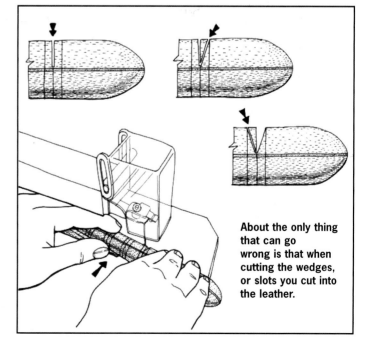

About the only thing that can go wrong is that when cutting the wedges, or slots you cut into the leather.

CUTTING LIST

	LENGTH	WIDTH	THKNS
Inner side (2)	300mm	66mm	8mm
Inner end (2)	300mm	50mm	8mm
Inner top (1)	66mm	66mm	8mm
Outer side (2)	300mm	82mm	8mm
Outer end (2)	300mm	64mm	8mm
Outer base (1)	82mm	82mm	8mm
Lipping (1)	650mm	8mm	3mm
Inn blocks (2)	50mm	50mm	8mm
Out blocks (2)	66mm	66mm	8mm
Top mirror (1)	70mm	50mm	3mm
Base mirror (1)	74mm	74mm	3mm

Amaze a child or grandchild with this extending periscope, that lets you look that little bit higher.

HOW TO MAKE A PERISCOPE

Prepare or buy enough 8mm thick material for all the pieces. This is a good project for using up offcuts.

1 Prepare the four side pieces for the bottom section and cut the slot for the locking knob. The bolt is glued into the knob and the nut into the periscope side. A morticer will do the job easily although a coping saw and file will suffice. Glue the four pieces together and use light clamping pressure.

2 Carry out the same procedure for the top (inner) section and remember to glue an M6 nut into the correct side using epoxy glue.

3 Glue the mirror blocks into position and cut the mirrors to size with a glass-cutter. Use a double-sided tape to hold the mirrors in place and check that the mirrors are properly aligned.

4 Glue on the top and base and sand flush with the sides. Set an M6 bolt into a piece of dowel for holding the periscope up.

For safety's sake, include two clear plastic windows (in case either mirror ever gets broken). Use a router to cut a rebate around the two mirror openings and drop the plastic windows into place. A small mitred lipping holds the plastic in place securely.

5 Finish off with a light sanding, particularly on the corners and edges. Wax, but note few treatments will protect the toy from children at play!

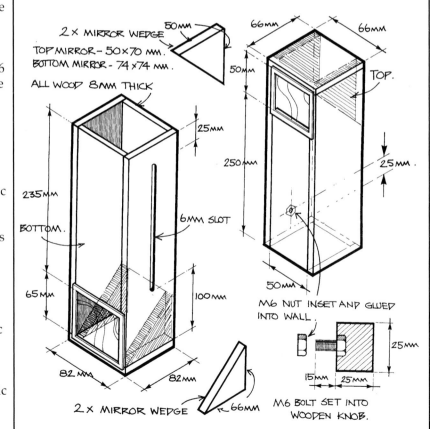

2× MIRROR WEDGE
TOP MIRROR – 50×70 mm.
BOTTOM MIRROR – 74×74 mm.
ALL WOOD 8mm THICK

50MM

66MM   66MM

TOP.

25MM

250 MM

25MM.

235MM

BOTTOM.

6MM SLOT

100MM

65MM

50MM

M6 NUT INSET AND GLUED INTO WALL.

82 MM   82MM

2× MIRROR WEDGE

66MM

25MM

15MM   25MM

M6 BOLT SET INTO WOODEN KNOB.

Make a small rocking horse for young children

This project was made from birch but you may want to use ply or MDF for a larger version. You could even paint MDF.

HOW TO MAKE THE ROCKING HORSE

1 Start by cutting out the head and seat. These are joined to one another with a kind of halving joint. You cut interlocking slots in the head and seat so that the two pieces slide together. You could easily change the shape of the head into that of a dinosaur or big cat if riding lions attracts.

Pick the grain carefully for the head. Avoid any short grain around the ears, which can easily snap off. Choose close-grained pieces. Drill the head for the dowel handle.

2 Cut the runners to shape. You may need to experiment with the curve on the runners to ensure the rocking motion is smooth. Use a spokeshave, files and rasps to cut back any bumps and then sand the runners smooth.

3 Cut out the two spacers (D) that join the runners together.

Make sure the spacers are exactly the same width for consistency.

4 Smooth all the curves on the seat. Remove all sharp edges so that they cannot hurt a young child.

5 Cut the slots in the head and seat. These need to be interlocking. The fit must be snug but not too tight. Cut the slots with a bandsaw, jigsaw or tenon saw, chiselling or sawing away waste.

6 The rocking horse is held together with screws and glue. The screws are hidden by plugs, so you will need to counterbore all the holes first for plugging.

7 Start assembling the horse by screwing the front spacer to the head. These screws will be hidden so only really need to be countersunk.

8 Now you can screw (and plug) the runners to the two spacers ensuring the runners are even.

9 Now that you have the head, runners and spacers joined together you can add the seat. Do this by screwing down into the runners, and then fitting plugs.

10 Sand the plugs smooth and wax the horse.

CUTTING LIST			
	LENGTH	WIDTH	THKNS
A Seat (1)	432mm	225mm	25mm
B Runners (2)	673mm	140mm	25mm
C Head (1)	315mm	225mm	25mm
D Spacer (2)	100mm	90mm	25mm
E Handle (1)	190mm	15mm	15mm

Cut out the head and the runners with a jigsaw or on a bandsaw. They will need cleaning up

Cut the slots in the head and in the seat so that they can interlock. It must be a snug fit

Assemble the rocking horse and fit the plugs. Make sure the grain is in the right direction

HOW TO MAKE A JUNIOR WORKBENCH

1 Draw the shape of each component onto sheets of MDF and label each piece with a soft pencil for future reference. The bench has been designed to keep waste to a minimum.

2 Use a portable jigsaw to cut out the parts. Use a fine-toothed blade to reduce any tearing and to make your job easier when planing the edges square. If you can, get an extra pair of hands to help you support the wood.

3 It is important to plane all the edges of the MDF square, to help form good strong joints. With MDF you must be prepared to sharpen your plane blade often. Jointing should pose no difficulty: the workbench only needs to be glued and screwed, and cramps are not required.

Drill 2mm (⅛in) pilot holes and 3.5mm (5/32in) clearance holes, and finish off with a countersink. The main frame is fixed together with 38mm (1½in) No 6 twin-thread woodscrews and Resin W PVA adhesive for extra strength. When the frame is dry, the screw heads must be below the surface of the wood. Fill the holes with a wood filler.

4 Fixing on the top strengthens the frame and takes the stress off the corner joints. Use four woodscrews to hold the top in place. Again, it is good practice to strengthen the joint with adhesive. Glue and nail the two raised tops in place, forming a tool well and covering up the screw heads that hold down the top.

5 Glue and screw the shelf in place on the inside of the legs.

This reinforces the lower frame and provides a storage area for a tool box.

6 Plane and sand off any sharp edges. This is essential: there must be nowhere for young woodworkers to bump heads, nor screw tops or nail heads for them to cut themselves on.

If you choose to paint some areas of the bench, use a hard-wearing and non-toxic (acrylic) paint. The brighter the better. Wax-polish any unpainted MDF surfaces to prevent grubby marks from little fingers!

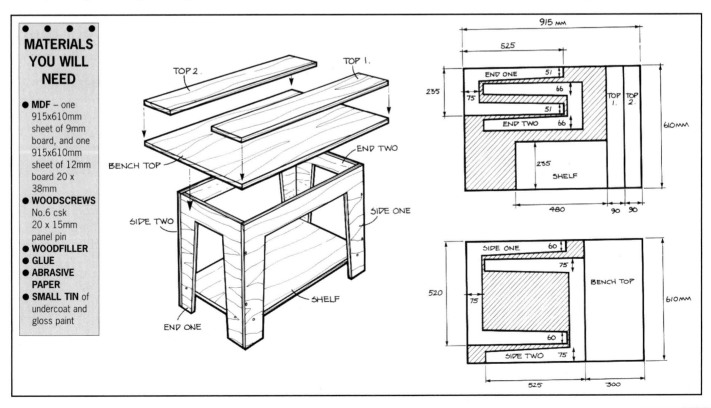

MATERIALS YOU WILL NEED

- **MDF** – one 915x610mm sheet of 9mm board, and one 915x610mm sheet of 12mm board 20 x 38mm
- **WOODSCREWS** No.6 csk 20 x 15mm panel pin
- **WOODFILLER**
- **GLUE**
- **ABRASIVE PAPER**
- **SMALL TIN** of undercoat and gloss paint

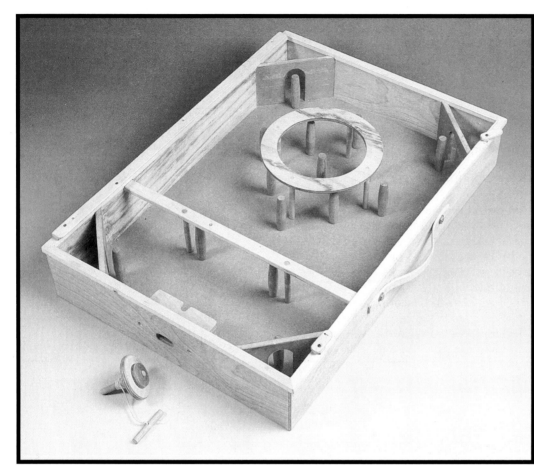

lipping for the rail that supports the two front posts. Having cut all the notches, nail and glue the lipping down, doing the same for the partitions. Screw a handle to the carcase for mobility.

4 Drill the cross-rail and the ring for the dowel posts, and screw up into the posts through the base.

5 For the lid, use 6mm (¼in) ply, and work a groove all along the frame rails. Cut little tenons on the end of the long rails to fit in the groove. All you then need is a rebated batten along the top of the arena carcase into which the lid slots, and turn-buttons on the opposite side to hold the lid down.

MARKING STARTING STALLS

6 Make the starting stalls separately, and then attach the unit to the carcase. Nail and glue two spacers between two pieces of ply, and cut a notch into the front edge of the upper

Make a game that combines skittles, pinball and spinning tops. Heavy tops spin longer than light ones, but the ones made of thinner ply are fastest out of the stalls. Some tops are so fast that they can leap out of the arena.

HOW TO MAKE THE ARENA

1 The bulk of the carcase can be made from plywood, with solid timber for the lippings and posts. Start by cutting the four sides to length and working lap joints on the ends of the long sides. Make the lap about two-thirds of the depth of the ply, then glue and nail the carcase up

square. It helps to tack on the thin ply bottom before the glue goes off to ensure it fits. Otherwise wait, nail on an oversize base and then plane it back flush.

2 Nail and glue a softwood lipping around the top edge of the carcase, with mitred corners, and a groove along the lower face the width of the sides and 6mm (¼in) deep. Before fitting the lipping, cut out the four corner partitions, with the ends mitred to 45°, and mark where they will go on the sides. Cut notches out of the lipping, to the depth of the groove, to take the top 6mm (¼in) off the partitions.

3 The notches stop the partitions sliding while you glue them in position with nails through the sides. You may also want to cut similar notches in the

and lower pieces to hold the tops. Fix this assembly to a ply backboard,with a hole for the string. Cut a corresponding hole in the carcase, and screw the stall to the end of the arena.

7 The shape of each top is determined by the position and shape of the starting stall. You can use 12mm (½in) dowel for the spindle, and one, or two, thicknesses of 10mm (⅜in) for the body.

8 Make the skittles either from 25mm (1in) dowel shaped with a block plane, or of course by turning

them. Mark their positions on the base of the arena. Thread a 760mm (30in) piece of string through some dowel, as a handle, and twist it neatly around the top. You may need to hold the arena down as you pull the string.

HOW TO PLAY TO THE RULES

One point is scored for every skittle knocked down in the middle of the arena, and three points are won for any corner skittles knocked into the arches. If you knock down all 15 skittles (scoring 23) in one turn you are entitled to another spin.

CUTTING LIST					
	MATERIAL	QTY	LENGTH	WIDTH	THKNS
A Side	Ply	2	900mm	130mm	12mm
B End	Ply	2	600mm	130mm	12mm
C Base	MDF	1	880mm	586mm	9mm
D Corner partition	MDF	4	200mm	120mm	12mm
E Circle	Ply	1	280mm	280mm	12mm
F Cross rail	Pine	1	580mm	22mm	19mm
G Skittle	Dowel	15	90mm	25mm	25mm
H Pins	Dowel	6	120mm	12mm	12mm
I Lid panel	Ply	1	800mm	526mm	6mm
J Top side rail	Pine	2	800mm	29mm	15mm
K Top end rail	Pines	2	572mm	29mm	15mm
L Body for tops	Ply	1	90mm	90mm	12mm
M Spindle for tops	Dowel	1	90mm	12mm	12mm

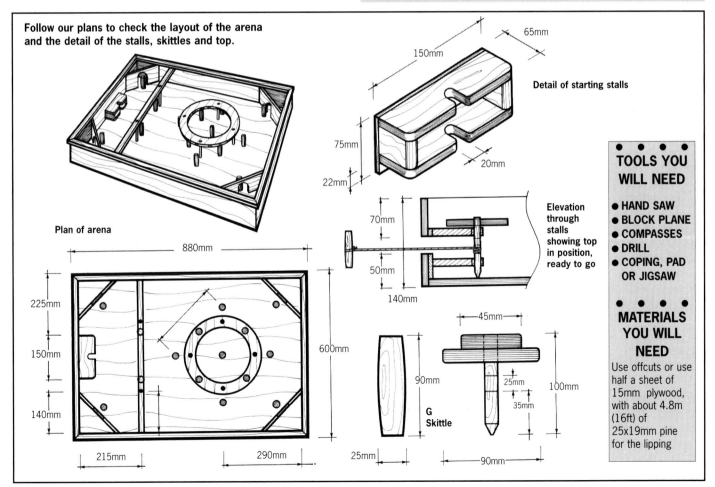

Follow our plans to check the layout of the arena and the detail of the stalls, skittles and top.

Detail of starting stalls

65mm
150mm
75mm
22mm
20mm

Plan of arena

880mm
225mm
150mm
140mm
215mm
290mm
600mm

Elevation through stalls showing top in position, ready to go

70mm
50mm
140mm

45mm
90mm
25mm
35mm
100mm
25mm
90mm

G Skittle

TOOLS YOU WILL NEED

- HAND SAW
- BLOCK PLANE
- COMPASSES
- DRILL
- COPING, PAD OR JIGSAW

MATERIALS YOU WILL NEED

Use offcuts or use half a sheet of 15mm plywood, with about 4.8m (16ft) of 25x19mm pine for the lipping

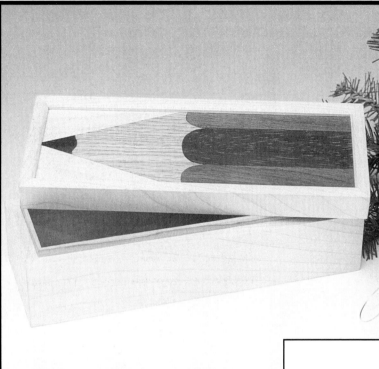

Cedar can be used for the bottoms and linings. Cut the bottom to size and insert both bottom and top into their grooves. To clamp the box lay the components corner to corner and stick lengths of Sellotape along the parts. This naturally tightens as you assemble the box. You can also use rubber bands to stop any movement.

5 After the glue has set, cut the lid from the base with a tenon saw. Mark round the box first, making sure the lines meet. Cut the linings and insert inside the base. Finish with fine sandpaper and wax. Decorate the top with veneers before assembling the box.

CUTTING LIST			
	LENGTH	WIDTH	THKNS
End (2)	75mm	60mm	8mm
Side (2)	200mm	60mm	8mm
Panel (2)	189mm	64mm	3mm
Lining (1)	500mm	34mm	2mm

Use one simple section to make a pencil box, with mitred corners, that can be designed to any shape.

HOW TO MAKE A PENCIL BOX

1 The trick with the pencil box, or any such geometric container, is to make the sides from identical setions which can be made in lengths for efficiency. Cut up enough timber for the sides and ends, and plane to thickness and width. Make sure you have enough length to account for the mitres and some excess.

2 Rout the grooves for the base and top. Note that these are the same width and depth, and are the same distance from the top and bottom edges of the stock. Bevel the inside face.

3 Mark the sides and ends to length and cut them at the required angle. It is easiest to cut them oversize and sand them to length with the correct angle using the table or a disc sander.

If you have a mitre saw it might well be accurate enough, but sanding machines are wonderful for this kind of task.

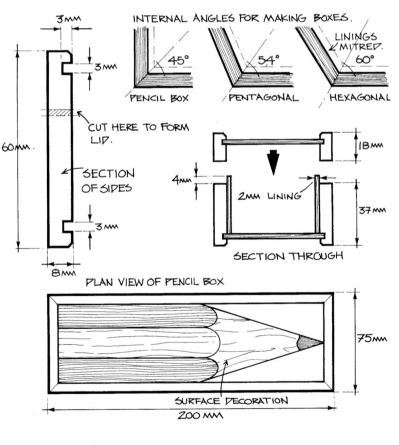

INTERNAL ANGLES FOR MAKING BOXES.

3MM

3MM

60MM

8MM

CUT HERE TO FORM LID.

SECTION OF SIDES

3MM

45° PENCIL BOX

54° PENTAGONAL

LININGS MITRED. 60° HEXAGONAL

18MM

4MM

2MM LINING

37MM

SECTION THROUGH

PLAN VIEW OF PENCIL BOX

75MM

SURFACE DECORATION

200 MM

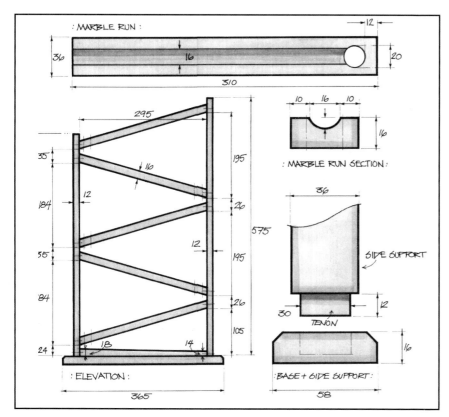

: MARBLE RUN :

: MARBLE RUN SECTION :

SIDE SUPPORT

TENON

: ELEVATION :

: BASE + SIDE SUPPORT :

CUTTING LIST			
	LENGTH	WIDTH	THKNS
A Long side	571mm	36mm	12mm
B Short side	495mm	36mm	12mm
C Track (5)	310mm	36mm	16mm
D Base	370mm	58mm	16mm
E Base track	296mm	36mm	16mm

How to make a wooden track for playing a new game with marbles.

HOW TO MAKE THE MARBLE RUN

1 Start by planing up the wood for the track. This is butt jointed, with screws, to the sides so cut the ends at an angle of about 15.° Remember that the angle goes the same way at each end. Make sure you rout the groove on the upper side of the wood.

2 The best way to form the groove is with a radius cutter and router. It is easiest if you can use your router in a table. It best to drill the hole through which the marble drops before you rout the groove.

3 Having routed the groove, drill the sides for the screws and fix them to the tracks. Screw and glue the base to the bottom of the sides. Sand the run very smooth, finish and find a marble to play.

If you have a radial arm saw you will doubtless know that cross-cutting is done so much more quickly if you cramp a temporary stop at one end. If you want, alter the angle of the run

Chamfer the edge of the base with a block plane for a classier finish. It is important to drill the marble holes before forming the groove, as the drill bit is difficult to centre otherwise

The quickest way to assemble the marble run is to screw the sides to the track. For a more elegant piece you could try dowels or even mortice and tenon joints

How to make fun people for children from offcuts.

NOSE

130MM HIGH.

ARM.

32MM SQUARE

HOW TO MAKE FUN PEOPLE

1 Close-grained hardwood, like beech, is ideal for the figures.

You will need blocks about 120mm long and 32mm square. Beech turns well and takes a nice edge for details.

2 If you intend to turn many people it is worth making a guide for the important features. Mount a blank between centres and turn to a 30mm diameter cylinder.

3 With your turning guide, mark the feature lines on the revolving blank. Use a small spindle gouge and skew to shape the figure.

4 Sand with 240 grit aluminium oxide abrasive paper, and finish with 400.

5 Remove the work and replace the headstock centre with a drill chuck to turn the arms from a length of 6mm dowel. Turn the nose from the same dowel.

6 File a flat on the inside face of each arm, and a matching flat on the side of the body. Glue the arms in position with PVA, and drill a 2mm hole for the nose. Cut out a shield (if appropriate) from thin ply with a coping saw and stick to one arm.

7 Paint the figure with acrylic paints, and then acrylic matt varnish to protect the colour.

If you intend to make many of the same people it is worth drawing up a guide template for marking on the feature lines. Diameters are proportional to each other

You may find it helps to dowell the arms to the body. If so, use bamboo barbecue skewers, available from supermarkets. Hold in a vice until the PVA glue sets

This is a far easier puzzle to make than it is to solve if you follow these step-by-step instructions.

The beauty of this puzzle is that it can be made to any size, and is the ultimate quick use for a waste piece of wood. A small pocket-sized version is about 10mm (3⁄8in) thick and a table-top one up to 20mm (3⁄4in).

HOW TO MAKE THE PUZZLE

1 Prepare one piece long enough for all three

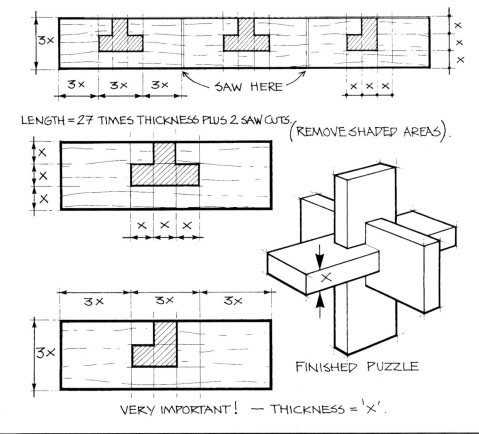

'X' CAN BE BETWEEN 10 AND 20 MM ACCORDING TO SIZE OF PUZZLE YOU WANT AND DETERMINES LENGTH AND WIDTH.

3x

3x | 3x | 3x   SAW HERE   x x x

LENGTH = 27 TIMES THICKNESS PLUS 2 SAW CUTS.

(REMOVE SHADED AREAS).

x
x
x

x x x

3x | 3x | 3x

3x

FINISHED PUZZLE

VERY IMPORTANT! — THICKNESS = 'X'.

parts and mark the waste using a try square, marking knife and gauge. The width is three times thickness, and length three times width.

2 Remove the waste when the length is complete, using a tenon saw, coping saw and chisel or alternatively you can cut the whole puzzle on a bandsaw or fretsaw. Accurate cutting is essential for the puzzle to fit.

3 Separate into the three puzzle pieces and sand down. Use an oil finish which will help the pieces to slide past each other.

Now see how many ways you can reach the solution to this interlocking puzzle!

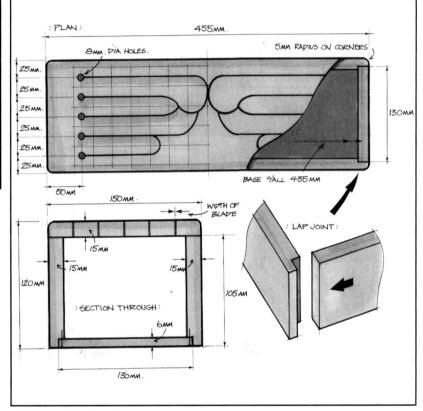

: PLAN : 455MM.

8MM DIA HOLES.

5MM RADIUS ON CORNERS

25MM.
25MM.
25MM.
25MM.
25MM.
25MM.

130MM

50MM

BASE O/ALL 435MM

150MM.

WIDTH OF BLADE

: LAP JOINT :

15MM

15MM   15MM

120MM

105MM

: SECTION THROUGH :

6MM

130MM.

The tongue drum must be one of the simplest musical instruments to make. By experimenting with the timber type and the dimensions of the tongues, you can alter the sound.

HOW TO MAKE A TONGUE DRUM

1 Start by planing up the stock for the sides, ends and top, all 15mm thick. Leave the material for the sides and ends all in one piece and then rout the rebate for the bottom.

2 Cut the sides and ends to length and then cut the laps on the ends of the sides. Use a tenon saw to cut the shoulder first and then chisel away the cheek.

3 Cut out the base from thin ply and also the stock for the top.

Mark out the shapes of the tongues on the top. Drill the ends of the tongues so that the wood does not split.

4 Cut the tongues with a jigsaw using a thin blade to get round the corners. Clean up the gaps with abrasive paper.

5 Assemble the box sides and ends. You can add the top at this stage, but do not fit the bottom. If you do, dust from finishing the top will stay in the box.

6 Glue the top to the sides and ends and trim it flush around. Round over the edges and sand smooth.

7 Make your own sticks with rubber balls on dowel.

Cut a rebate in the end of each side. Use a tenon saw first to cut the shoulder, and then pare away the waste with a chisel. Hold the piece down on the bench

Use a router to cut the tongue shapes. You can experiment with the shapes and sizes. Here ash was used but you could try other types of wood

CUTTING LIST

	LENGTH	WIDTH	THKNS
Side (2)	455mm	105mm	15mm
End (2)	130mm	105mm	15mm
Base	435mm	130mm	6mm
Top	455mm	150mm	15mm

What child can resist playing with a 'plane? Better still a helicopter with spinning rotor blades.

HOW TO MAKE THE HELICOPTER

1 Start with the body. This can be made from standard PAR timber from the timberyard. Hunt around and you'll probably find someone who can sell you offcuts.

2 Draw out the main body using a French curve for a smooth contour. Cut out the profile shape, but before removing the window, drill a 12mm dia. hole through the base of the body for the pilot. This avoids splitting when the drill exits. Seal the hole at the bottom with a 18mm dia. button or a 12mm plug.

3 Glue the wheel support stubs onto the body and do the same with the boom for the rear rotor. If you do not have a lathe you could use a plane to shape the boom roughly and then smooth it round with abrasive.

4 Clean up the body and varnish or colour to your choice using acrylic finishes. Decorate the pilot's face and glue into place firmly. You can turn the pilot, with a 12mm spigot on the end, alternatively just whittle it to shape, or use a sander to do so.

The wheel axles are 6mm diameter steel rod. Drill out the wheels and body for the axles (which go right through the body front and back) to give a loose fit. Retain the wheels with spring caps for a neat finish. You can produce the wheels on a lathe or with a holesaw. Screw the rotors to the body and boom. Finish the original helicopter with matt varnish, or give it a colourful finish using safe toy paints.

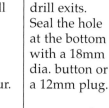

CUTTING LIST

	MATERIAL	LENGTH	WIDTH	THKNS
Body (1)	Pine	246mm	92mm	25mm
Wheel support (2)	Pine	63mm	32mm	16mm
Front wheel (2)	Mahogany	25mm	25mm	12mm
Back wheel (2)	Mahogany	41mm	41mm	12mm
Main rotor (1)	Oak	203mm	20mm	10mm
Rear rotor (1)	Oak	67mm	10mm	10mm
Boom (1)	Pine	120mm	22mm	22mm

If you have a lathe then turning the boom will be no problem, but otherwise you will need to shape it by hand with planes, etc... and smooth with abrasive

Fit the boom to the body with a spigot on the end of the boom. The wheel support stubs are simply butt jointed to the sides of the body before drilling the axle holes

The pilot fits into the 12mm diameter hole you drill up from below. You could easily use dowel instead of turning the pilot and its spigot

HOW TO MAKE A TOBOGGAN

1 Either select some 50x50mm (2x2in) prepared softwood (PAR) or buy it sawn and plane square. Cut it into six lengths - two 900mm (36in), two 300mm (12in) and two 150mm (6in) - for blocking up to make the runners. You'll also need an extra 460mm (18in) length to rip down the middle later to make the cross battens at the front and rear of the sledge.

2 Glue up the lengths of softwood to form two runners, with a nose at the front which can be shaped once the glue has dried.

Use Cascamite or a waterproof adhesive. Place both in G-cramps and leave to cure for at least eight hours.

3 Clean up the glued joints with a plane, then carefully draw on the shape of the runner. Cut to the line on the waste side with a jigsaw or bandsaw. If you use a jigsaw, make sure the blade is long enough to cut through 50mm (2in) thick wood.

4 Clean up the profile with a plane or coarse sanding block.

Trace the shape of the finished runner onto the other piece, shade the waste and cut to shape.

5 Measure and cut the 4mm (⅛in) plywood to size using a tenon or hand saw. You will need two pieces which will be glued to form a thicker laminate. Plywood bends more in one direction than the other, so make sure when selecting and marking out that it will go with the bend when you put it on the sledge. Cut one of the ply laminations from each of the pieces you have bought, using the waste for the thin strips that stop the user slipping on the sledge.

6 Spread glue on the top edge of one runner and tack the plywood flush with the end of the sledge using an 18mm (¾in) brass hardboard pin. Progressively pin the plywood to the top of the runner at 76mm (3in) intervals along the bend. Make sure there are no bulges. Squeeze the plywood firmly into the bend and continue tacking at shorter intervals, cramping as well. Repeat on the other runner. The pins will be hidden under the top plywood slats.

7 You should have ample waste ply to make the slats. Cut five 76mm (3in) wide strips and one 178mm (7in) wide strip, and clean up their edges with a plane and abrasive block.

8 Glue a batten onto the plywood at the front, anchoring down the large ply strip using glue and brass countersunk screws. Use G-cramps to secure it before drilling and screwing. Add the other strips, inserting extra pins or screws at the centres of each board to ensure a good glue join. Glue and screw another batten onto the plywood at the rear.

9 Make sure all screw heads are countersunk slightly below the surface, then clean up the edges with

2 Spread Cascamite evenly over one surface for gluing up the runner

3 Use G-cramps to hold the blocks in place as the glue sets

1 Cut the lengths of 50x50mm (2x2in) PAR into three for the runners

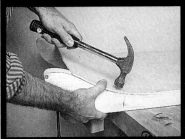
7 The ply will not be able to bend all around the curve of the runner

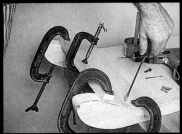
8 Screw and glue the wide ply and batten in place at the front

9 Cut a notch near the front of the runner so the threshold is flush

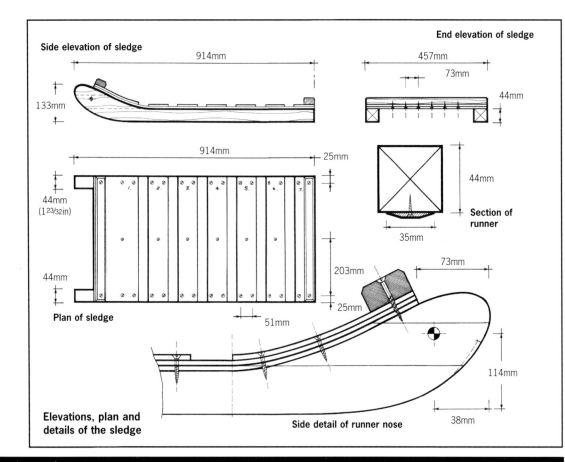

Side elevation of sledge

914mm

133mm

End elevation of sledge

457mm

73mm

44mm

914mm

25mm

44mm
(1 23/32in)

44mm

Section of runner

44mm

35mm

Plan of sledge

51mm

203mm

25mm

73mm

114mm

38mm

Elevations, plan and details of the sledge

Side detail of runner nose

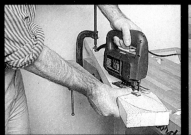

4 Cut the curve with a jigsaw, keeping to the waste side of the line

5 Having smoothed the curve, use the runner to mark out the second one

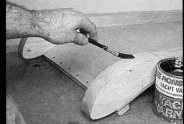

6 Thin ply can be cut with a tenon saw, but check the grain direction

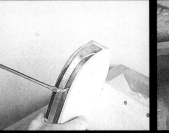

10 Screw the aluminium strip in place, countersinking the screws

11 Finish with as many coats of yacht varnish as possible, leaving to dry

12 Drill the hole for the rope, not too close to the end of the runner

a plane to ensure the plywood is flush with the runners. Bevel or soften all edges with a sanding block.

10 Cut a nick in the runners at the top of the curve to take the end of the aluminium strips flush. Screw down one of the threshold strips, which are about 38mm (1½in) wide, into the nicked position and carefully coax it around the bend. A piece of scrapwood might help here. Screw it down as you go until you reach the end, then repeat with the other runner.

11 Select some stout cord and drill holes at the front of the runners, countersinking the holes to soften their edges. Then take the runners off again and clean up the entire sledge ready to paint or varnish.

12 To varnish, apply several coats to get a high gloss finish. Allow half a day and rub the sledge down between coats.

13 Replace the aluminium strips, making sure that all the screws are countersunk slightly below the surface of the metal, to reduce the risk of cutting tobogannists in the snow.

Discover how to make this classic game without a lathe.

HOW TO MAKE THE SOLITAIRE BOARD

1 Plane up the base of the board.

2 Cut the piece of veneer and glue to the base. Make sure the glue is evenly spread and that the pressure gets to the centre as much as the sides. Leave it to dry overnight.

3 Cut the board to a square, making sure the sides are exactly square to one another by measuring across the diagonals. If the measurement from one corner to another, across the diagonal, is not the same the piece cannot be square.

4 Start the marking out and drilling with the four outside lines. You actually have to do remarkably little marking if you can set up a fence on your drill press. All you need to know is the distance between the centres of the dimples. You will really only need two settings for the fence. There are 33 holes to be cut in all. Of those 24 will be cut on the first four outer lines. You then only have nine holes to drill along the two central lines.

5 Mark out three lines each way on the square. The trick is then to fit a thin drill bit in the chuck of your drill (held in a drillstand). You use this to position the fence accurately for drilling. Offer the square up to the fence, which you adjust until the drill bit is central on the line. If you are holding a small router in a drillstand, you will need a very fine cutter for this style of adjusting the fence. Now you can replace the drill bit with a coving cutter (sometimes known as a core box cutter). It may not be ideal using a router cutter in a drill, as the speed is low, but the only problem ought to be a rough finish, and that can be solved relatively easily.

DRILLING THE MARBLE HOLES

6 Drill the outer holes, neatly spaced apart. Once you have drilled the first row of seven holes, spin the square through 90° and do the next. Repeat this, and then reset the fence to drill the last nine holes on the two central rows.

7 The trouble with using a router cutter at a slow speed is that the finish is poor. Clean up the dimples with an abrasive cutter.

Be really careful not to let the bit be in contact with the wood for too long or it will burn and scar the surface. Of course, both the finish and burning can be solved by using a router in the drillstand. This will need guards or featherboards to keep the work secure.

8 Having drilled and cleaned up the holes, turn the square over and use a compass to mark out the circle. You can then cut that roughly to the line with a jigsaw. Then fit a drum sander in the pillar drill, and screw the board to a base so that it can revolve for cleaning up. Then use a router and bevel cutter to cut the bevel around the outside.

CUTTING LIST			
	LENGTH	WIDTH	THKNS
A Base (1)	195mm	195mm	20mm
B Veneer (1)	195mm	195mm	0.6mm

Mark out the grid of lines on a square piece of wood. Then align the outer lines with the fence by putting a small bit in the chuck and using that for centring

Use a jigsaw, bandsaw or fretsaw to cut the board roughly to shape. The better the cut now the less work you will have to do later!

Screw the board to a false base, and position it close up against a drum sander held in a drillstand. Revolve the board to sand it circular

This ice cream van is specially designed to take a Touch-n-Play unit. You can also personalise your van to suit the potential owner.

All you will need is some 3mm, 6mm and 9mm ply, a few ½in pins, glue and four wheels.

HOW TO MAKE THE ICE CREAM VAN

1 Begin by cutting out the two sides and the floor. Mark the position of the floor on the sides, 7mm above the bottom edge, and then pin and glue the floor between the sides. The front edge of the floor is flush with the front ends of the sides.

2 Cut the internal divisions and the rear from 9mm ply. Glue the rear into position between the sides. Do not shape the curve at this stage. Add the triangular fillet to the inside top edge of the rear. Add the seats and the seat backs, and paint these and the cab side of the division. Then glue the partition into place. Complete the turning of the interior. Prepare and fit the bonnet.

3 Cut a 1in wooden wheel in half for a steering wheel. Stick it to the dashboard and paint them both matt black, then sand the bonnet to the side profile, and glue in the windscreen frame (from 3mm ply). Use woodfiller to make the curve between the windscreen and the bonnet.

4 The roof is in two parts, with the top made of 9mm ply, and the false ceiling of 3mm. Cut the ceiling to fit snugly between the sides. Drill a hole in the roof for the Touch-n-Play music unit, then glue the ceiling underneath the roof, with a central 3mm hole in the ceiling, which needs to be painted before fitting.

5 Round off all the edges, except at the bottom, and sand the van smooth. Then add the front bumper, made of 9mm ply. The easiest way is to cut back the front of the van, from the wheel arch forwards, and then add the bumper to protrude a little.

6 The wheels revolve on a length of ⅛in brass tube, and are retained on 14SWG spring caps attached to the ends of a length of 14SWG wire, position through the centre of the tube. The tube is retained by the axle supports. Cut the supports from 9mm ply and drill the ⅛in holes for the tube. Glue the supports to the floor. Push a length of tube through the holes and place a wheel on each end. Mark and cut the tube so that it protrudes a fraction from the wheel centres. Fit a spring cap to one end of a length of 14SWG wire and feed the wire through the brass tube. With the cap tight against the end of the tube, mark the wire that protrudes so there is just enough to take the second spring cap. Cut the wire and fit the cap.

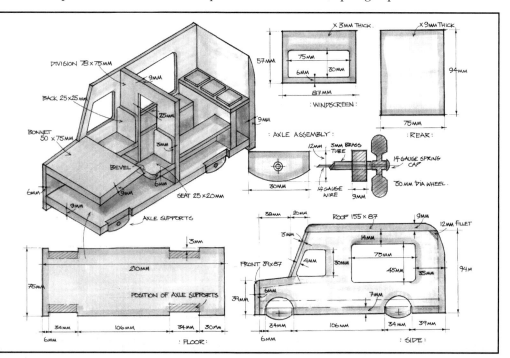

7 After painting the body, rule on the doors with Indian ink, protected by a thin coat of varnish. Use Letraset or Edding rub-down transfers. These can be rubbed directly onto the van. Use self-adhesive labels for the stickers.

8 Finally glue the Touch-n-Play unit into the hole in the roof. The 30mm wheels are part WHL2, and spring caps are HC14.

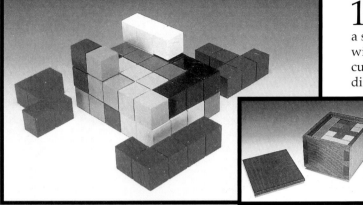

HOW TO MAKE A RECTANGULAR PUZZLE PIECE WITH A BOX FOR STORAGE.

A pentomino is a collection of five squares joined together at the edges. A set of pentominoes is a collection of 12 of these. The set can be assembled so that they interlock to form various sizes of rectangles.

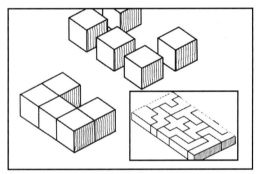

There are a number of rectangles you can produce with 12 pentominoes.

Make each pentomino from five separate cubes. Cut 60 cubes, each one 20mm (13/16in) long from a piece measuring 20x20x 1260mm (13/16 x 13/16 x50in).

1 Mark the length of one cube onto the wood using a set square and then cut with a tenon saw. Mark and cut one cube at a time as it is difficult to make allowances for the width of the sawcut if they are all marked out before sawing begins. Smooth the end-grain using a disc sander or by hand.

2 To make the pieces the blocks are glued together. Hold them in place with rubber bands whilst the adhesive sets and then smooth using a couple of grades of glasspaper.

3 Prime the wood using a primer / filler spray, which fills in any flaws. It is necessary to re-emphasise the lines where the cubes are joined together using a fine-toothed saw as they are also filled in by the spray.

4 The colours used are acrylic paints for artists. Apply them with a brush, then spray on an application of clear lacquer.

MAKING THE BOX
There are more than 3000 ways of putting them in the box, but it is difficult to believe when trying to find just one.

BOX CONSTRUCTION
1 The four sides, two short (B) and two long (A), are cut to the correct length.

2 Using a set square, mark a line 12mm (½in) in from the ends of each piece across the width of each side. This is the area where the pins and tails are marked and cut.

3 Mark the tails on the short sides using a dovetail template.

4 Cut the tails with a tenon saw and then a coping saw to clear the waste.

5 After the tails are cut, identify and mark corresponding corners. Each

Mark out the cubes on a length of square wood. Using dividers is a quick way to mark equal divisions

Glue up the pentominoes with PVA wood glue, holding the cubes together with elastic bands

Once the glue has set clean up the joints and paint the pieces with acrylic paints and then varnish

set of pins is marked from a set of tails that might vary slightly and identifying the corners would prevent mistakes during assembly.

6 Having done this mark the position of the pins on the ends of the long sides, from the tails on the matching ends of the short sides.

7 Cut the pins using the same methods used when making the tails.

8 Fit all the joints together to check for accuracy and adjust if necessary. When the fit is satisfactory, the joints are glued, assembled and the diagonals checked to ensure the box is square before the

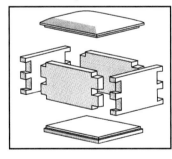

adhesive sets. Clamp the box lightly in this position.

9 After the adhesive sets, plane flat the top and base of the assembly, and clean all the joints using a smoothing plane.

10 Cut the lid (C) to size and indicate the position of the rebates. This is done by placing the sides centrally over the lid and drawing around the insides of the box onto the underside. Then form the rebates using a rebate plane.

11 The base of the box (D) is made using the same methods as the lid, but when finished it is glued into place.

12 Round the top of the lid using a smoothing plane and glasspaper.

13 Finish the box using medium and smooth glasspaper. Wet the wood slightly to raise the grain and smooth again with 00 grade steelwool. This is

followed by three applications of polyurethane clear matt varnish, rubbed down using steelwool after the first two coats. The final stage is to apply several coats of wax.

VARIOUS SOLUTIONS

One way of solving the puzzle is to make a rectangle with 10 squares on one side and six on the other. This example is only one of the many solutions to the puzzle of fitting the shapes into a rectangle, but there are several

hundred more, all of which are quite difficult to crack.

CUTTING LIST					
	MATERIAL	QTY	LENGTH	WIDTH	THKNS
A Long side	Hardwood	2	130mm	76mm	12mm
B Short side	Hardwood	2	109mm	76mm	12mm
C Lid	Hardwood	1	130mm	109mm	12mm
D Base	Hardwood	1	117mm	97mm	12mm

Cutting lists always give the full length of a piece including the joint, but not wastage. Allow at least 25mm extra for length and 5mm on the width and thickness of sawn stock

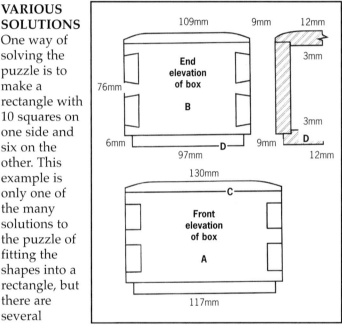

MAKING THE DOVETAILED BOX

Cut down the waste side of the lines with a tenon saw, and then remove the waste with a coping saw

Use the tails on the short sides to mark the pins on the long sides. Also mark the pin depth

The lid and the base are let into the sides. Rebate the lid and base with a rebate or shoulder plane

How to make a toy farm from MDF taking advantage of the speed of a glue gun.

Both barn roofs lift off, giving access to the tractors. The drop-in centre lid doubles as a field and pond and lifts off. A flat lid means it can be stored, taking up as little room as possible when not being played with. If you plan to paint the farm you need non-toxic paints.

HOW TO MAKE THE FARMYARD

1 Mark out all the pieces on the ply or MDF and cut out using a hardpoint saw. Gently sand the edges.

2 If you have a router, rebate the outside walls at the bottom edge to take the base panel. Do the same to the top inner walls of the two barns to provide a ledge for the roofs. If you do not have a router you could just glue some thin battens to the sides of the walls to hold up the roof.

3 Cut out the doors, windows, entrance and barn arches with a powered

Details of the toy farm

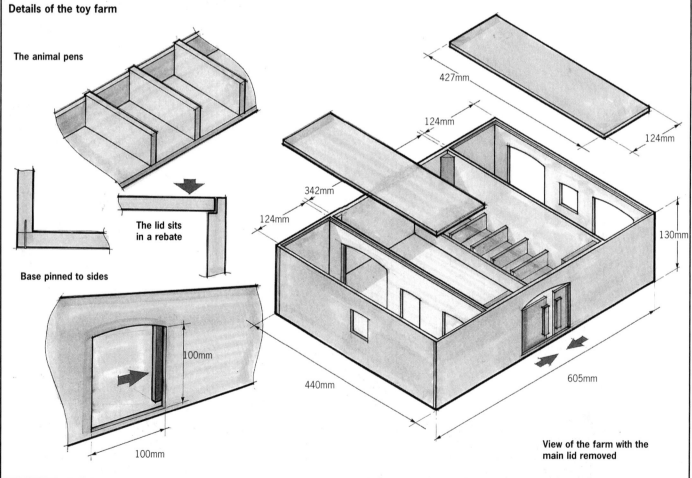

The animal pens

The lid sits in a rebate

Base pinned to sides

100mm

100mm

427mm

124mm

124mm

124mm

342mm

124mm

130mm

440mm

605mm

View of the farm with the main lid removed

fretsaw or coping saw. Check that the barn arches and the front entrance are wide and high enough for a tractor, or even a combine harvester!

<table>
</table>

CUTTING LIST			
	LENGTH	WIDTH	THKNS
Ends (2)	440mm	130mm	6mm
Front and back	605mm	130mm	6mm
Internal wall (2)	430mm	130mm	6mm
Base (1)	600mm	430mm	6mm
Barn roof (2)	427mm	124mm	3mm
Centre lid (1)	425mm	342mm	3mm

Use 6mm and 3mm MDF or ply. Dimensions given for butt jointing. If a router is used adjust dimensions accordingly

4 Glue (with PVA glue) and pin the outside walls, the base, and the internal barn walls. Reinforce the corners with triangular blocks in the centre section to support the main lid.

5 Make a row of animal pens from offcuts glued to a base. Borrow some animals to get the size of the pens right.

6 Make runners and cut two sliding doors from offcuts for the entrance.

7 Drill finger holes with a ¾in Forstner sawtooth drill in each of the roof pieces to aid lifting out. Then lightly sand and prime the whole farm with white acrylic primer.

8 Paint and decorate the farm with acrylic paints and brick paper as required. Remember to leave enough clearance for the paint so that the lids and doors fit. Secure the animal pens in position and make a little nameplate for the young owner.

The main central lid doubles as fields. You need to drill finger holes for pulling it off. You can rebate the top of the walls for the lid, or glue on supporting battens.

With the barn roofs removed you can see the space for the machines. The doors must be wide enough for a tractor, plough, baler and harrow

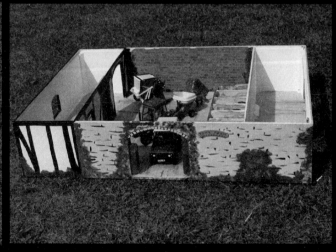

Fit runners either side to keep the sliding doors in place.

holding the cheeks in a vice. A pillar drill is best but you have to be able to hold the wood, which will try to spin. You could of course drill this hole first and then use a jig with a stationary disc sander to make the cheek round.

4 Assemble the cheeks on a long piece of dowel

without glue.

Hold the dowel in the chuck of a power drill. Turn on the power drill and hold yo-yo against an abrasive pad. Take the dowel out of the chuck and glue up the yo-yo. You can use a slip knot to attach the string, which needs to be pretty tough. Away you go.

Find out how to make a yo-yo, attaching the string with a slip knot.

The grain needs to be running across the central axis. This version has been made by cutting out circles on the bandsaw and then sanding them round, with a dowel in the centre.

HOW TO MAKE THE YO-YO

1 Start by planing up a piece of hardwood for the cheeks. Try a variety of thicknesses. Mark out the circles with compasses, though you might want to make a template if you intend to make lots more yo-yos.

2 Cut out the cheeks with a bandsaw, jigsaw, fretsaw or coping saw.

3 Drill the hole for the centre

Elevations of a wooden yo-yo

2mm

54mm — 8mm

54mm — 20mm

54mm

End elevation of yo-yo

Dowel spindle

8mm

42mm

Side elevation of yo-yo

Start by cutting out the two cheeks from a piece of hardwood. It helps to have a bit of weight, but avoid making too heavy a yo-yo for children

Drill the cheeks for the dowel and assemble the yo-yo so that the spindle can be fitted into a drill chuck. Then you can power sand the yo-yo smooth

CHAPTER 2

GIFTS

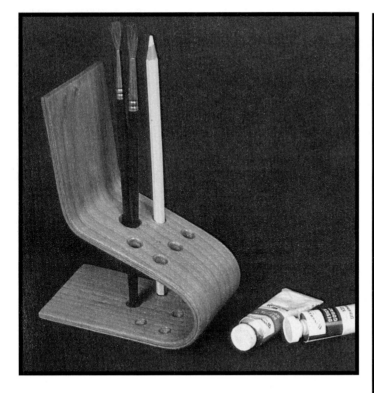

You can rout the first layer freehand, and then use it as a template for the other parts of the former, with a guide bush screwed to the router base

Screw the bottom layer of the former to a base and then screw and glue each layer on top of the first. Try to keep all the edges flush

Use the original former as a way of holding the piece while you drill and coutersink the holes for the pensils or brushes you plan to store

An innovative project that incorporates shape with lamination.

HOW TO MAKE THE BRUSH HOLDER

1 This holder needs no more than one leaf of veneer, and some offcuts of chipboard. The cherry veneer that has been used for this project is about 6ft long and 250mm (10in) wide, and 0.6mm thick. You need to cut that into strips about 64mm (2½in) wide and 360mm (14in) long.

2 Mark out the curve you want on a piece of chipboard, and with a router and straight cutter, cut to half depth. Separate the two pieces with a jigsaw, turn them over and clean up the edges with a guide brush and cutter. Use these as templates for cutting the other layers of the former again with a guide bush and straight cutter.

3 Now you can screw and glue the layers together, making sure they line up, but first screw the bottom layer to a baseboard. With this shape you must be careful that the cramps do not make the formers slide. When gluing up ensure the cramps are at an angle to the base of the holder and not square to it.

4 Once set, use one of the formers to hold the shape while you clean up the edges with a block plane, and then drill and countersink the holes for the brushes.

This prop has five slats. Three of these support your book, and the other two pivot back as legs. The front three (A) are joined by a shelf, and the legs (B) by a foot.

HOW TO MAKE THE BOOK PROP

1 Start by planing up the timber for the slats (A and B). They are all the same thickness and length. If you intend to use a radiused router cutter for rounding over the top of the slats then the thickness must match the radius of the cutter. You are better off keeping the ends square for the moment so that you can hold them squarely against a fence for drilling.

2 Use a pillar drill or drill-stand for the pivot hole. You'll only be able to drill one slat at a time, so the quickest way to go about it is to set up the fence for repetitive work. If you then cramp a stop to the fence you do not need to mark up each slat. Start, as you would for drilling the dimples in the solitaire board (See Project No.14 page 26.), by marking the hole centre on one of the slats. Then put a fine drill bit in your drill chuck and bring it down just into the wood. Then you can adjust the fence to suit, and also add the stop. Now all you have to do is butt each slat against the fence and stop, having changed the fine fit for a larger one, to suit your dowel. You may find that you have to sand down the dowel a fraction to make it fit in the hole smoothly. When it comes to drilling the holes, do so from both sides, to meet at the centre, otherwise there is bound to be breakout. It is worth positioning the stop on the fence so there is a fair amount of waste beyond the hole.

You can rout and sand the excess away, but if you try drilling too near the end you do risk breaking the short grain there.

3 Once you've drilled the pivot holes you must clean up the slats and drill the screw holes for fitting

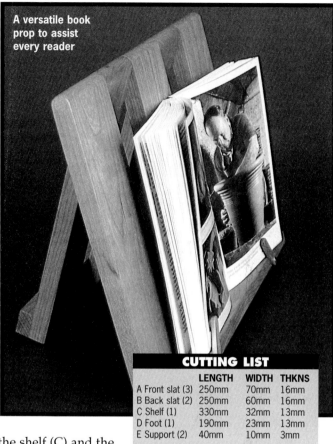

A versatile book prop to assist every reader

CUTTING LIST

	LENGTH	WIDTH	THKNS
A Front slat (3)	250mm	70mm	16mm
B Back slat (2)	250mm	60mm	16mm
C Shelf (1)	330mm	32mm	13mm
D Foot (1)	190mm	23mm	13mm
E Support (2)	40mm	10mm	3mm

the shelf (C) and the foot (D). You can also bevel the bottom of each slat so that they sit flat on the surface when open. You can stick rubber pads along the bottom edge to stop the prop slipping.

4 Run the dowel through the holes, and glue into the outer slats. Screw on the shelf and foot, and then add the little supports at the front to keep your book open.

Start by drilling the holes for the dowel hinge. Use a pillar drill, with a stop to keep the holes consistent

Tap the dowel pin into the slats, gluing it in place at each end. Make sure it is not too tight

You need a pair of supports at the front of the shelf to stop your book from closing inadvertently

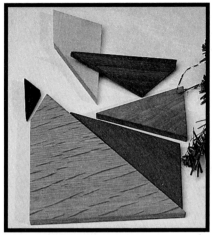

This is a clever dissection of a pentagon into six pieces which can also form a square. It is a real brain-teaser. This puzzle is unsuitable for young children.

HOW TO MAKE THE PENTAGON PUZZLE

1 Stick the paper templates onto the wood and cut them out. The thickness of the wood doesn't matter but somewhere between 5mm and 15mm is ideal. Finish the pieces on abrasive boards and wipe the surfaces with a little Danish oil.

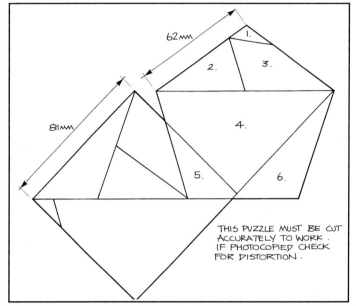

THIS PUZZLE MUST BE CUT ACCURATELY TO WORK. IF PHOTOCOPIED CHECK FOR DISTORTION.

Laminated geometric shapes make excellent earrings.

HOW TO MAKE PAIRS OF EARRINGS

1 Start by gluing up any pattern of contrasting woods, using offcuts and bits of veneer. Produce lengths as long as you need.

They can always be stored away for another day. Try to get the meeting surfaces as smooth as possible for a good bond. Use PVA glue and as many cramps as you need. Leave to set overnight.

2 When set, clean up the faces of the block to reduce work later.

3 Finishing is best done on wet and dry abrasive paper glued onto pieces of 25mm (1in) MDF. Use 120, 240 and 400 grit boards and then finish the earrings with beeswax. Sand one surface of the earrings prior to slicing from the block and grip the other with a blob of Blu-Tac, whilst sanding on the boards.

4 Use hypoallergenic earring posts, with butterfly clips, stuck in place with epoxy resin glue. The posts are available from craft shops. Make sure no excess glue gets onto the inside surface of the posts as it can cause skin irritation to the wearer. With the appropriate fittings you could also make cuff-links.

Plan and side elevation of earrings

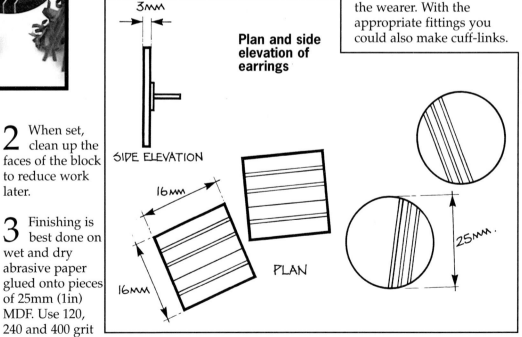

SIDE ELEVATION

PLAN

Find out how to make a clock by fitting an inexpensive quartz movement into a recess in a solid piece of timber.

Cutting the outer shape of the clock is simple, either by hand or with a bandsaw or fretsaw, but making the recess for the movement is a little trickier. To make the cutting of the recess easier, we chose to use a round movement. That way you either drill out the recess or turn the hollow on a lathe. If you choose the latter technique, you will need to make a chuck for holding the body. You will also need then to cover the mechanism. To achieve the best grain match on the back you will want to cut a slice off your original block of wood and later shape it to fit the recess.

HOW TO MAKE THE CLOCK

1 Start making the clock by preparing the blank slightly deeper than required and then cut off a 3mm (⅛in) thick slice to be used for the back cover.

2 The most difficult operation is the cutting of the circular recess for the quartz movement. A Forstner bit is the quickest way, although you would

first need to use a larger bit to cut the shoulder for the cover.

A faceplate jig for the lathe gives the best results because you can turn the shoulder for the cover using a small scraper. The chuck takes the 89x70mm (3½x2¾in) blank and is positioned so the centre lines up exactly with the clock spindle. You can then turn the recess for the

clock or use a Forstner bit held in the tailstock. Make sure the clock fits and that the hands can move freely. Glue in place if it does not have a retaining nut.

3 Cut the top of the clock on the bandsaw and sand. Cut and fit the back cover and secure it with two small brass screws. Finish the clock with 400 grit abrasive and wax applied with 0000 wirewool.

CUTTING LIST

	LENGTH	WIDTH	THKNS
Body	89mm	70mm	42mm
Mechanism (1) Junghans quarts W739 Available from mail order suppliers and clock suppliers			

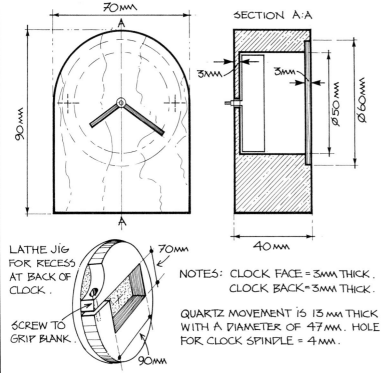

SECTION A:A

NOTES: CLOCK FACE = 3MM THICK.
CLOCK BACK = 3MM THICK.

QUARTZ MOVEMENT IS 13 MM THICK WITH A DIAMETER OF 47MM. HOLE FOR CLOCK SPINDLE = 4MM.

LATHE JIG FOR RECESS AT BACK OF CLOCK.

SCREW TO GRIP BLANK.

These are perfect gift ideas that take no time to make.

HOW TO MAKE THE ANIMAL BROOCHES

1 Start off by photocopying and enlarging these templates and stick them on to the pieces of wood with Pritt Stick. Alternatively, design your own templates.

It is easier to make several brooches at once by using wood 15mm (19/32in) thick.

2 Cut out the pieces with a fretsaw and stick them together with fast setting epoxy resin glue.

3 Glue the finished assembly onto a large block of wood. When it is set slice off as many brooches as you can with a bandsaw or tenon saw. This makes holding easier and much safer.

4 Glue the brooch pins on to the backs of the brooches with epoxy adhesive. The pins are available from craft shops and craft mail order suppliers. Make sure the pin is slightly higher than the centre of the brooch to stop it from falling forward.

5 Use abrasive boards to clean up the front surface and finish with wax, applied with 0000 wirewool.

Enlarge to 117% on a photocopier (beware of distortion)

PUFFIN

DUCK

PENGUIN

SWAN

GOOSE

Play around with laminating and weaving by making a hair slide from a selection of veneers.

HOW TO MAKE A TEMPLATE

1 Transfer the template to 25mm MDF to make the laminating former. Cut the MDF into the two parts and line the edges with plastic or Sellotape to prevent glue from sticking to them.

2 The laminated hair slide can be made from almost any veneer.

The outer layer will show the most and so this is the place to use some special veneer, some marquetry or

THE EXTERNAL DIMENSIONS OF FORMER ARE NOT IMPORTANT – BUT THE CURVE IS! WHEN PLAN IS ENLARGED, IT FITS THE SHAPE OF THE TOP OF THE HEAD.

HAIRSLIDE PIN

HAIRSLIDE FORMER – 25 MM THICK MDF.

120 MM

SUGGESTED WIDTH OF SLIDE = 25 MM.

THICKNESS – 7 VENEER = 5 MM.

Enlarge on the photocopier to 11.8mm squares

CUTTING LIST			
	LENGTH	WIDTH	THKNS
Hair slide (5)	115mm	22mm	0.6mm
Hairpin (1)	125mm	5mm	5mm
Weave (2)	980mm	5mm	0.6mm

some contrasting woven veneers. Always use an odd number of veneers with the grain running in the longest direction for strength. Glue up with Cascamite (don't use PVA) and leave clamped in the former for 24 hours.

3 Drill and shape

two holes to take the hairpin. You need to know the thickness of a bundle of the recipient's hair and this in turn depends on the hairstyle. This determines where the two hairpin holes are drilled. One end of the hairpin must be tapered or pointed.

4 If you decide to weave the outer layer, make a piece of weave larger than you need with thin strips of veneer. Glue it down onto the hair slide with PVA spreading the glue thinly. Once dry you can trim the weave flush with a scalpel.

5 Sand the hairpin and hair slide but only wax the outside surfaces.

CUTTING LIST

	LENGTH	WIDTH	THKNS
Side (4)	100mm	45mm	6mm
Lining (1)	370mm	28mm	2mm
Top (1)	96mm	96mm	4mm
Base (1)	93mm	93mm	3mm

HOW TO MAKE THE JEWELLERY BOX

1 Prepare a 450mm long strip of wood planed to width and thickness. Use a marking knife to score the lengths of the sides and cut to length with mitres.

2 Sand down to the knife line, whilst holding the wood against a mitre guide on a sanding disc, for the most accurate joint.

3 As to the method of gluing up, lay out the sides, inside face downwards, and stick Sellotape along their length. As you pull the joints together the tape tightens. Remember to fit the base on assembly.

4 Prepare the top. This can be plain, laminated or decorated. If you do use marquetry, note that it will thicken the top. Glue the top into place and leave.

5 Mark around the carcase of the box once it has set and then separate the top from the bottom with a tenon saw.

Sand the edges flat on an abrasive board. Cut the linings, and glue into place. Sand with fine abrasive and finish with 0000 wirewool and a wax polish.

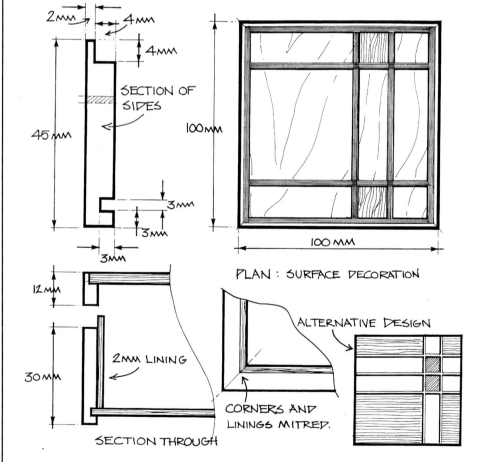

SECTION OF SIDES

PLAN : SURFACE DECORATION

2MM LINING

ALTERNATIVE DESIGN

CORNERS AND LININGS MITRED.

SECTION THROUGH

This miniature chest of drawers is a simple housing joint and mitring exercise. The housings are short and can easily be cut by hand with a chisel and saw. You do not have to stop them at the back, which makes cutting easier.

HOW TO MAKE THE MINIATURE CHEST

1 Start the chest by preparing the two sides. Cut the stopped housings with a tenon saw and chisel or use a router. Cut the grooves for the back panel; a combination plane or router is ideal.

Cut the four dividers to length and glue the main carcase together. Use the back panel to help in keeping the assembly square; locate it in the grooves and pin it in the middle to the top and bottom cross pieces.

2 Cut the two lippings to cover the housings on the front edges and glue in place. Cut or buy the mouldings for the top and bottom of the chest. Some of the smaller pine mouldings from DIY shops are ideal. Glue the mouldings into place, using clothes pegs as clamps.

3 The top can be plain or a moulding can be routed around the top edge. Glue the top to the top surface of the mouldings. Make the drawers as you would the jewellery box (see page 40).The knobs can be turned or bought from a DIY shop.

jewellery box (see page 40).

4 Finally, sand and wax the miniature chest.

The drawers for the chest are so small that they can be mitred. Use a router for moulding the top and apply mouldings around the base and under the top.

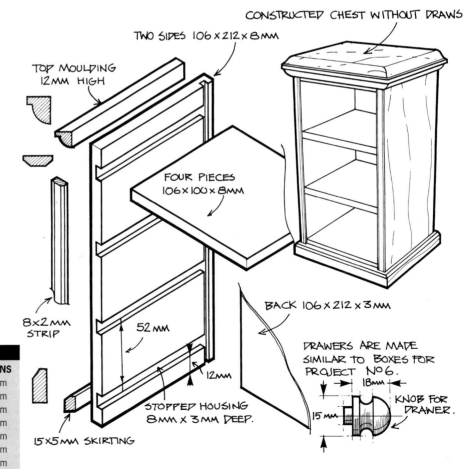

CONSTRUCTED CHEST WITHOUT DRAWS

TWO SIDES 106 x 212 x 8MM

TOP MOULDING 12MM HIGH

FOUR PIECES 106 x 100 x 8MM

8 x 2 MM STRIP

52 MM

12MM

STOPPED HOUSING 8MM X 3MM DEEP.

15 x 5MM SKIRTING

BACK 106 X 212 x 3MM

DRAWERS ARE MADE SIMILAR TO BOXES FOR PROJECT No 6.

18MM

15 MM

KNOB FOR DRAWER.

CUTTING LIST

	LENGTH	WIDTH	HKNS
Side (2)	212mm	106mm	8mm
Divider (4)	106mm	100mm	8mm
Top (1)	135mm	117mm	8mm
Back (1)	212mm	106mm	3mm
Drwr side (12)	100mm	100mm	8mm
Drwr base (3)	90mm	90mm	3mm
Skirting (1)	380mm	15mm	5mm

USE AS TEMPLATES FOR TREE DECORATION

Make sure your tree has an individual feel by making your own decorations from offcuts

If you are going to use opaque paints to decorate the decorations, the choice of timber doesn't matter; 3mm thick sycamore cuts well without splintering and the pale colouring shows through the paints. Use these templates by enlarging the shapes on a photocopier and tracing around them.

HOW TO MAKE TREE DECORATIONS

1 Cut out the templates and stick them onto the wood with Pritt Stick. Cut along the lines - an electric fretsaw is a lot quicker than a coping saw, and a jigsaw will probably be too clumsy. Drill the holes for cord and make sure they will hang level.

2 Clean off the Pritt Stick, sand and paint. A coat of matt varnish will help to make them last a few years longer.

CHECKLIST

1 Trace from the plan
2 Cut out tracings
3 Place wood to thickness
4 Stick templates to wood
5 Cut out shapes
6 Paint and varnish with acrylics

A stylish storage holder for spaghetti.

1 Start by setting up a sliding bevel set to 22.5°. Cut the sides to the widest width then place the bevel, checking regularly with the sliding bevel.

2 Then cut off the shorter lengths for the lid.

Rebate both ends of the lid, parts for the top and to fit over the tongue on the base of the container. Rebate the sides of the body, but note that the rebate is on the outside at the top and on the inside at the bottom to take the base piece.
Check the rebates on the lid and base pieces marry up correctly. Assemble the sides and cut out MDF or wooden pieces for the top and the base. Champfer the edges on the top piece and then glue them both in place and finish with oil or wax.

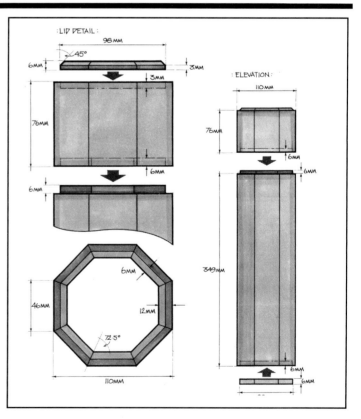

: LID DETAIL :
98 MM
45°
6 MM
3 MM
3 MM
76 MM
6 MM
6 MM

: ELEVATION :
110 MM
76 MM
6 MM
6 MM
349 MM
6 MM
6 MM

6 MM
46 MM
12 MM
72.5°
110 MM

How to make a mirror by hand or by using a router or even a lathe, and standard bevelled mirror glass.

HOW TO MAKE THE HANDLED MIRROR

1 Start making the handled mirror by sticking a template onto the wood with Pritt Stick or Spray Mount. Cut out along the line with a bandsaw and carefully smooth the edge to a precise and smooth series of curves.

2 Mark the circle for the mirror recess with a pair of sharp dividers to score the wood a few millimetres deep.

3 Use the router by hand to rout out to the

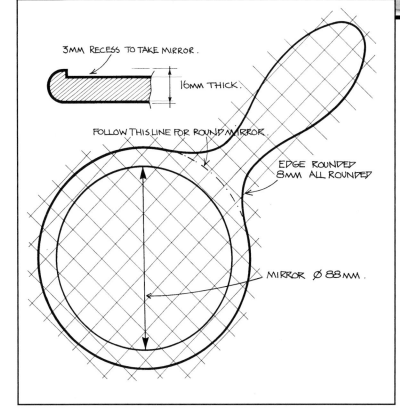

3MM RECESS TO TAKE MIRROR.

16MM THICK.

FOLLOW THIS LINE FOR ROUND MIRROR.

EDGE ROUNDED 8MM ALL ROUNDED

MIRROR ⌀ 88MM.

CUTTING LIST			
	LENGTH	WIDTH	THKNS
Body (1)	210mm	105mm	16mm
Mirror (1)	88mm	88mm	8mm

depth of the mirror, approaching the circumference of the circle cautiously.

4 Run the router around the perimeter of the mirror with an 8mm radius cutter. Once you have finished the top surface, turn over and start the bottom edge but check first that the bearing on the cutter will still run around the half-radiused edge.

This should leave you with very little sanding to do; finish off by giving the mirror two coats of wax and then glue the mirror into position.

5 Turn the round mirror, gluing a small spigot onto the back and holding this in a chuck. Part off and sand. Mark out the mirror, and cut to shape. Rout the recess for the mirror having marked the circle with dividers. Then round over the edges from both sides with a rounding over bit.

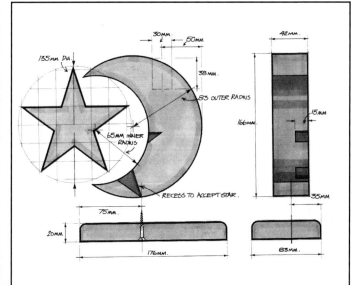

the moon. Remove the waste with a chisel holding the moon shape on the bench with a cramp.

4 Glue the star in the moon and screw the moon to the base.

Add some festive spirit to the Christmas table with this unique candlestick.

HOW TO MAKE THE CHRISTMAS CANDLESTICK

1 Start by drawing out the parts, to make card templates. You may well want to make more than one candle holder.

2 Now cut out the moon shape. If you have a bandsaw then you may need to make relieving cuts across the crescent, so that you can get the blade around the curve. You might find it easiest to drill the candle hole before cutting the outer curve. An abrasive flapwheel is excellent for cleaning up inside the curve.

3 Next cut out the star and use it to mark out, when making the notches in

Draw a template and cut out the moon using relieving cuts on a bandsaw

Chop out the notches for the star with chisels, taking care of the short grain

To drill the candle hole cramp the moon to a fence to keep it rigid

You might find it easiest to adjust the star to fit the notches with a file

How to make a present for the cook with these simple springing tongs.

HOW TO MAKE THE FOOD TONGS

1 You can make the top of the tongs to any shape. Make a template of the

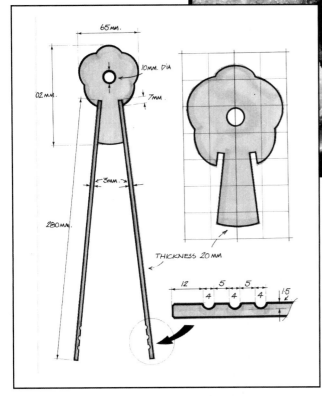

Use a round file to produce the grooves at the end of each arm for gripping. You may need to experiment with timber thickness to get the correct spring

shape and copy that onto the wood for the top.

This one is a bit like a shamrock.

2 Cut out the shape with a bandsaw, jigsaw or fretsaw. Drill a hole at the centre for hanging up the tongs. Cut the sides of the top for the arms of the tongs, making sure you cut little notches at the top of the sides for the rams to fit into.

3 Plane up the stock for the arms and use a round file to make gripping grooves near the end. Experiment for the right spring.

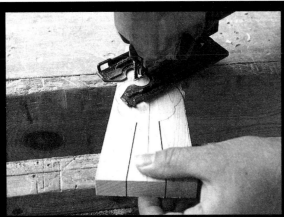

Use a jigsaw to cut out the shape for the top. Make sure the sides are straight

Glue and cramp the arms to the top on a flat surface so that the arms don't slide

How to make an octagonal mirror with contrasting maple and walnut

MAKE THE MIRROR

1 Start by gluing a strip of walnut to a strip of maple for the mirror frame. This can be a simple butt joint. Plane and clean up the joint when the glue has set.

2 Rebate the walnut part for the mirror glass on the back and chamfer it on the front. You can do this later with a router, but it produces rounded corners, which as you can see, are not as good looking.

3 Cut the strip into eight parts, with the mitres at 22½°. It is important that these are accurate, so use an adjustable set square to mark out and check the angles. You can use a mitre saw for this job, but you can make up your own special mitre box.

4 Biscuit join the eight pieces together. You could use a loose ply tongue easily enough. Cramp up with a strap cramp, having drilled two parts for the dowel pivots. Position these holes centrally to balance.

5 Cut out the base (A) and two supports (B). Drill for the pivots. Fix 3mm glass mirror in the frame with a ply back and pins, and then screw and glue the supports to the base with the mirror in place.

Though making this vanity mirror is simplified by the use of a router and biscuit jointer, it can easily be made by hand.
Equally you could make it from pine or a contrast of maple and American walnut.

CUTTING LIST			
	LENGTH	WIDTH	THKNS
A Base (1)	294mm	150mm	20mm
B Support (2)	140mm	124mm	13mm
C Outer (8)	203mm	31mm	20mm
D Inner (8)	177mm	19mm	20mm

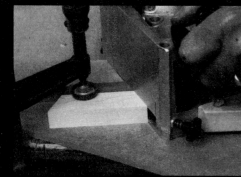

Having glued the two strips together the best way to join the sides is with a biscuit jointer

The biscuits help to locate the pieces and increase the gluing area. Most biscuits are too large so have been positioned so that the excess is rebated away

If you do not cut the rebates before assembling the frame you will have to do so with a router, using a rebating cutter and guide bearing

This frame rolls up the fabric. It has a bird's mouth adjustment that uses the springiness of the wood to hold the holding batten.

HOW TO MAKE THE EMBROIDERY FRAME

1 Start by preparing the stock and then cut the holding battens to length. These fit into the side rails with dowels. So as not to have to turn the ends, drill them to take a short piece of dowel. Drilling into end-grain can be difficult, especially if you need to get the dowel spot on straight. Cramp the batten parallel to the front of your bench and then drill with a flatbit, and use the bench as a guide.

2 Glue in the dowel and then round over the edges of the batten.

You can easily do this by hand with a plane, or alternatively, use a router in a table with a rounding over bit. Make sure the wood is well sanded.

3 Now move on to the side rails. Prepare the wood and start work on the bird's mouth. Mark out the position for the notch and then mark the bolt holes. Now drill the bolt holes so that they come near the end of the rail.

4 Drill the two holes in the bird's mouth. The furthest from the end of the rail is designed to stop the rail splitting. The other is for the dowel on the holding batten.

5 Now you can cut out the V that lets you hold the dowel with a bolt. Use a tenon saw, jigsaw or bandsaw for this, but keep it tidy.

6 Now fit the two feet that hold the frame up. Do this with a bolt and wingnut so that you can adjust the feet easily and hold them in place.

Make an adjustable needlecraft frame

7 Finally tack a piece of webbing to the holding battens, to which fabric can be stitched.

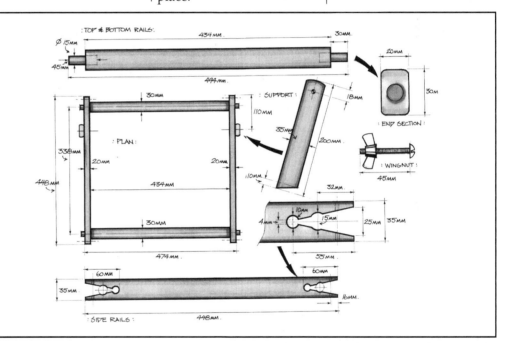

Drilling into end-grain to insert the dowel into the holding battens can be tricky. Cramp the batten to your bench and use the bench edge as a guide for direction

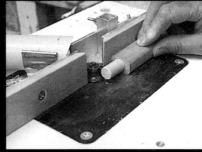

Smooth all the edges with a rounding over cutter or just a hand plane and abrasive. You should use a pushstick, and spring guards or featherboards

Finally add the short feet or legs. You can adjust the length of these to suit your needs. Bolt the legs to the frame, using a wingnut for easy adjustment

checking first that it is square by measuring the diagonals.

4 Make the top and bottom from two pieces of wood. For jointing, mark across the two pieces for a register, and true the edges on a shooting board. Plane one piece face down and the other face up to ensure any discrepancies in the set-up are balanced. Glue one edge and rub them together for about 10 rubs.

5 Glue on the top and bottom with a 1mm overlap all round. Clamp and tighten gently at both ends. Clean up the ends and then cut in half with a dovetail saw or a thin slot cutter mounted in a router.

6 The pin in the hinges and catch is made of 3mm (1/8in) ramin dowel, available from model shops.

TOOLS YOU WILL NEED

- ● DOVETAIL SAW
- ● BLOCK PLANE
- ● 6MM CHISEL
- ● SCALPEL
- ● SQUARE
- ● RULER

HOW TO MAKE THE BOX

1 Plane the front, back and ends to the right thickness and cut the ends to length. They must be shorter than the finished width of the box by the depth of the rebates. Cut the front and back overlength by 1mm and mark on the rebates.

2 Cut the shoulder on the rebates with a saw and chop out the waste with a

chisel. Alternatively use a router under a table. You can keep the workpiece square to the cutter with a T-jig. Cut a recess the same width and depth as the workpiece under the limb of the T, into which the piece fits. Back the piece into the router slightly to stop breakout at the end of the cut, then work against the rebate about two-thirds the depth of the timber. This maximises the gluing area

without diminishing strength.

3 Glue up the carcase, using elastic bands to hold it as the adhesive sets,

CUTTING LIST					
	MATERIAL	QTY	LENGTH	WIDTH	THKNS
A Front and back	Pine	2	198mm	58mm	6mm
B Ends	Pine	2	94mm	58mm	6mm
C Top and bottom	Pine	2	198mm	98mm	4mm
D Hinges and	Lignum	3	42mm	20mm	9mm

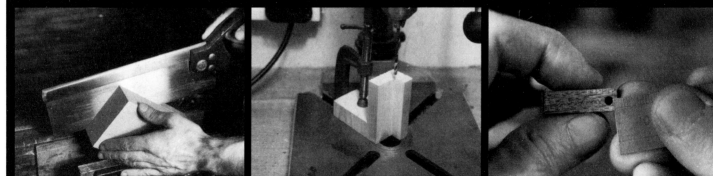

When cutting the lid from the base use thin wedges to stop the saw binding or making marks

Make a jig to hold the hinge and catch blanks upright as you drill the pin holes with a 2.8mm bit

The hole for the hinge pin must be positioned 1.5mm from the end to get the right clearance

Even using a pillar drill and jig it is difficult to drill a perfectly vertical hole due to the drill bit wandering slightly. The blanks for the catch and hinges are left oversize to allow for correction by planing after drilling.

7 Make the hinges and catch from two bits of timber. When drilling and planing is complete, round over the end with a router cutter or by planing and sanding. The hole must be 1.5mm from the rounded ends.

8 Mark in 6mm (1⁄4in) from the end for the interlocking knuckles. Shape the knuckles with the aid of a saw, chisel and scalpel. The central portion must be

double the width of the sides. Insert the dowel, then cut the piece up to form the different components of the hinge and catch.

9 Mark out the recesses for the catch and

hinges, making sure that the pin is positioned with the edge of the box and the division of lid and base running through its mid point. That means the recess has to be exactly 3mm (1⁄8in) deep. Use a scalpel for

marking as softwood is especially easy to crush.

10 Hold the box together with masking tape as you cut the recesses with the scalpel. Glue the hinges in place and clean up.

MATERIALS YOU WILL NEED

● **THIN SOFTWOOD** or hardwood offcuts

● **HINGES**
Lignum vitae is not easy to obtain but any other close grained timber will do. Try to have a colour contrast

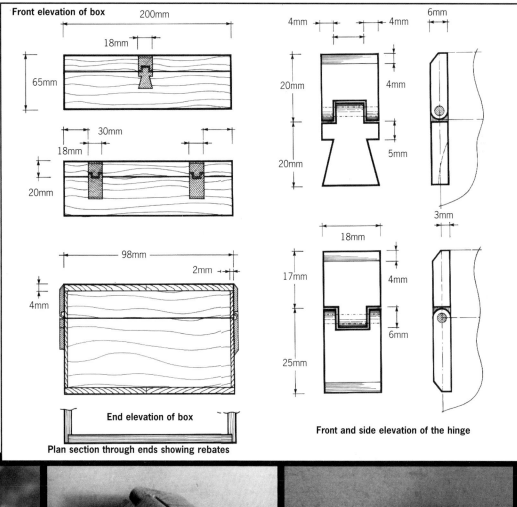

Front elevation of box — 200mm — 18mm — 65mm

18mm — 30mm — 20mm

98mm — 2mm — 4mm

End elevation of box

Plan section through ends showing rebates

4mm — 4mm — 6mm
20mm — 4mm
20mm — 5mm
3mm

18mm
17mm — 4mm
25mm — 6mm

Front and side elevation of the hinge

Work two hinge halves from one piece. Cut the other halves from grain consistent with the first pair.

Insert the pin into the double hinge without glue, so that it is a firm fit, but does not split the wood

Cut the double hinge in half with a fine dovetail saw to produce the hinge pair ready for fixing

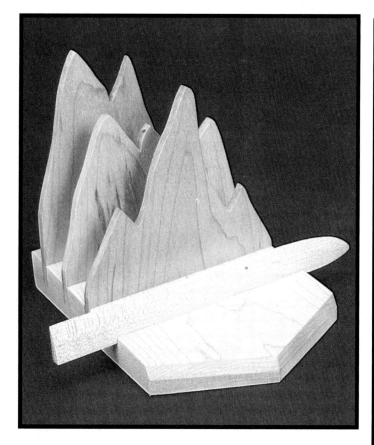

1 The quickest way to taper the rack base is with a jig in a thicknesser. For such a small piece it will not take long to plane the taper by hand

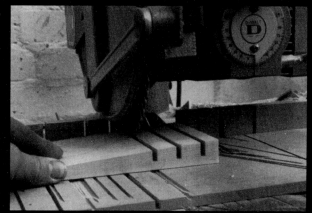

2 Again the technology of a radial arm saw speeds up the grooving, but this can easily be done with a tenon saw for the shoulders and chisel for waste

3 Cut out the divider shapes with a coping saw. Try to make use of any mountainous grain. Draw out the shape first to get the best shape before cutting

A quick way to make an intriguing rack for post.

Try to pick wood for the dividers that has a contour grain. That is why maple works well.

HOW TO MAKE THE RACK AND KNIFE

1 Cut out the base and plane the taper and chamfer. Then cut the grooves for the dividers, and the shallower groove for the knife. Note that the grooves are at right angles to the bottom of the base, not angled.

2 Cut out and plane the dividers, selecting the grain carefully.

Cut to shape, imitating the mountains. Stick the dividers into the grooves and leave the glue to set. Wax polish.

3 Cut out the knife and shape the taper with a belt sander or just by hand. Wax.

CUTTING LIST			
	LENGTH	WIDTH	THKNS
A Base (1)	160mm	120mm	21mm
B Divider (3)	134mm	120mm	5mm
C Knife (1)	1903mm	19mm	5mm

CHAPTER 3

HOUSE AND HOME

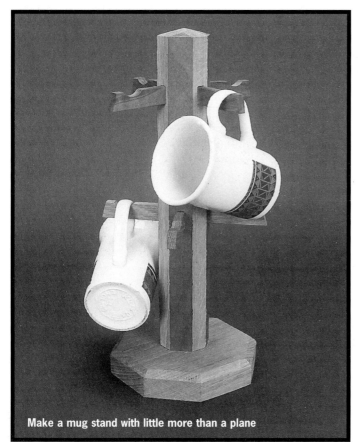

Make a mug stand with little more than a plane

2 When you are satisfied they are all square you can glue them up. If you do this all in one go you will need a packing piece on each side to hold the assembly together as you start cramping. These protecting blocks have to be just narrower than the sides of the rack. Use PVA adhesive, making sure there has not been any slip during assembly.

3 The wooden hooks can be cut from offcuts. Cut shoulders on one end to form a tenon (to match the chisel you use for the mortices). Use a drill or a coping saw to make the curved notch of the hook. Use a drillstand for drilling if possible, with a fence.

4 Cut out the base and chisel out the mortice in the centre. Remove the waste with a drill. Then

bevel the edges with a plane, and start planing the stem of the rack. Once octagonal you can chisel out the mortices for the hooks. It is, in fact, best to cut the tenon to suit the mortice.

HOW TO MAKE THE MUG RACK

1 Plane up nine lengths of contrasting wood so they are all 23mm square. If you have a planer-thicknesser you will, of course, be doing this with long lengths, but by hand it is easiest to plane shorter pieces.

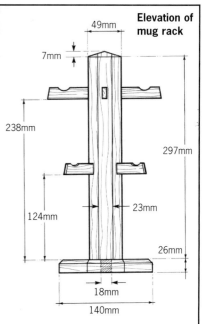

Elevation of mug rack

49mm
7mm
238mm
297mm
23mm
124mm
26mm
18mm
140mm

Making the mug rack is a planing and chiselling exercise. You can either glue up the nine square strips in one go, or glue up three layers one at a time

If the central strip is left overlength it becomes the tenon for fixing the stand. Use a drill to make the curves on each mug hook

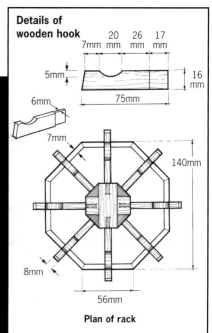

Details of wooden hook

20 mm 26 mm 17 mm
7mm
5mm
16 mm
75mm
6mm
7mm
140mm
8mm
56mm

Plan of rack

A multi-purpose bathroom accessory that no respectable bather can do without.

HOW TO MAKE THE BATH SHELF

1 Plane up the sides (A) and rails (B). Mark the mortice positions in the sides, and cut them with a chisel. If possible cut from both sides to ensure there is no breakout. Cut the curve at the end of each side and then sand with a foam filled abrasive drum.

2 Cut the rebates in the rails before cutting to length. Note the central rails have a rebate top and bottom, facing opposite directions. It is very easy to assemble these the wrong way. Cut the tenons on the rails (B), marking them out so that the ends of the tenons (horns) are a fraction too long. You can always plane them flush later.

3 Assemble the shelf (without glue first to check it over) and cramp it up. Use a watertight PVA adhesive or Cascamite and leave in cramps overnight, having checked for squareness.

4 Cut the slats to length, having planed them first, and then drill and countersink them at each end. Take the carcase out of the cramps and screw the slats in place with brass screws. Use an oil to finish.

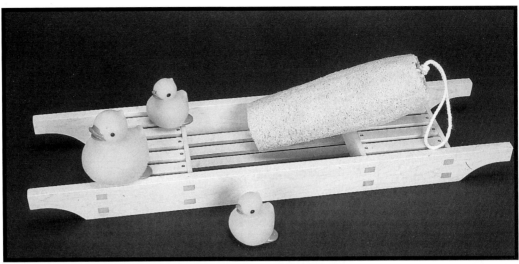

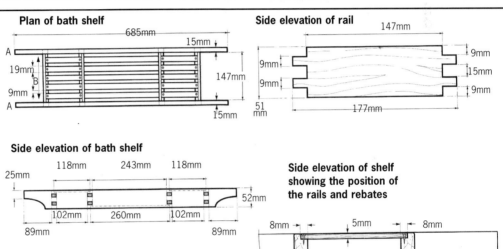

Plan of bath shelf — 685mm — 15mm — 19mm — 9mm — 147mm — 15mm

Side elevation of rail — 147mm — 9mm — 9mm — 9mm — 9mm — 15mm — 9mm — 51 mm — 177mm

Side elevation of bath shelf — 25mm — 118mm — 243mm — 118mm — 52mm — 102mm — 260mm — 102mm — 89mm — 89mm

Side elevation of shelf showing the position of the rails and rebates — 8mm — 5mm — 8mm — 15mm — 15mm — 5mm — 5mm — 8mm — 70mm

Having cut the mortices in the sides, rebate the rails and fashion the tenons to fit. Take the width of the mortices from the thickness of the rails.

Dry assemble the slides and rails on the shelf and measure the length of the slats. Remember that the central rails are handed, so position carefully.

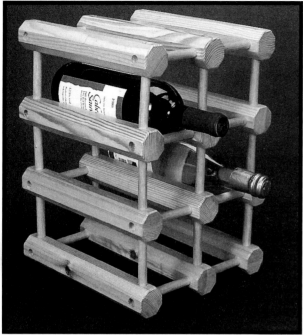

Details of wine rack

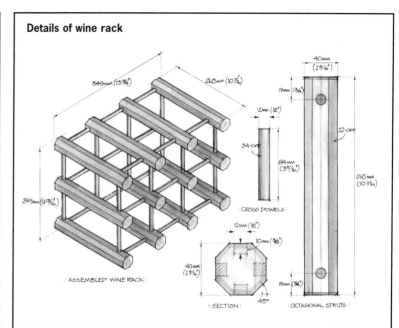

349mm (13¾")

265mm (10⅞")

249mm (9¹³⁄₁₆")

: ASSEMBLED WINE RACK :

12mm (½")

34-OFF

84mm (3⁵⁄₁₆")

CROSS DOWELS

40mm (1⁹⁄₁₆")

19mm (¾")

12-OFF

265mm (10⁷⁄₁₆")

12mm (½")

10mm (³⁄₈")

40mm (1⁹⁄₁₆")

45°

: SECTION :

19mm (¾")

: OCTAGONAL STRUTS :

A simple rack for bottles using prepared softwood and dowel.

HOW TO MAKE THE WINE RACK

1 Start by planing your stock square. If you've bought it prepared (PAR) it should be fine, but always check it first. Then remove the corners by hand with the plane, or using a thicknessing jig.

2 Set up a fence and a stop on the pillar, drill and drill all the holes, the same distance away from the ends.

3 Now cut the dowels to length, using a stop, and sand the ends smooth.

The dowelling needs to be a close fit in the holes for strength

If you have a thicknesser make a V cradle so that you can remove the corners quickly and accurately

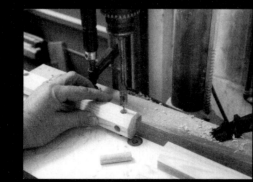

Hold the racking pieces against a fence and the stop to drill the holes with a spade bit

Saw the spacers to length with a tenon saw, again using a fence and stop for consistency

HOW TO MAKE THE SOAP DISH

1 Start by gluing up the two boards A + B. Because the dish is bound to get wet it is probably best to use Cascamite rather than PVA as it tends to be more waterproof in the long run.

2 Once the glue has set you need to clean up the faces and edges. It may seem a little pointless to plane it into a brick when it is likely to end up as bullion, but there is no sense in using the fence of a plane or a machine if your surfaces are not straight and square. It is a well-respected fact that good woodworking needs good registers.

3 Start by cutting the grooves in the top of the dish. You'll need a radiused cutter for this. Such a cutter is often known as a core box cutter. It has straight sides but a convex tip.

The grooves get narrower and shallower as you move from the centre. If you have one suitable cutter you'll have to do this by moving the fence a tad.

4 Start with the central groove. You ought to be able to cut the groove with one pass. If the router is labouring under the task make shallower cuts. If you are using a router, set it up in a table for ease. Now move the fence away a little and pass the workpiece over the cutter in both directions so that you cut on both sides of the initial groove. Then lower the cutter a bit and move the fence to cut the next two grooves. Adjust the cutter and fence again to cut the outer pair of grooves. Those outer grooves will look narrower than the next pair because they are deeper. The graduation in the grooves makes the dish look more interesting. Now turn it over and cut the two grooves on the underside. These are supposed to give the impression of feet under the dish.

5 Now you can start work planing the edges of the dish to give it that extra bit of shape. Preferably do the ends first so that you can plane away any tearing of the grain. Cramp some scrap to the long edges when planing the ends, so that there is less risk of breakout. Set up a sliding bevel so that you can check the angle.

6 Clean up the grooves. Roll a piece of abrasive paper around thin dowel or scrap to sand the grooves along their length.

7 Finally sand away the dish at the centre in which the soap sits. One way to do this is with a flapwheel in a drill. Taking care as you go. Varnish.

An attractive wooden dish for soap made with the minimum of tools

CUTTING LIST

	LENGTH	WIDTH	THKNS
A Top (1)	115mm	74mm	15mm
B Bottom (1)	122mm	80mm	22mm

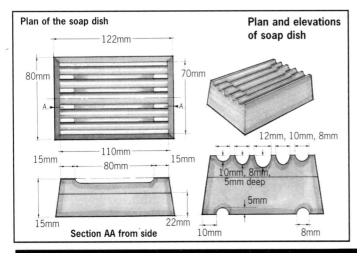

Plan of the soap dish
122mm
80mm
70mm
A. — A.
110mm
15mm | 80mm | 15mm
15mm | 22mm
Section AA from side

Plan and elevations of soap dish
12mm, 10mm, 8mm
10mm, 8mm, 5mm deep
5mm
10mm | 8mm

A router table is the easiest way to work the grooves on the top and bottom of the dish

Plane the edges on the angle after you have cut the grooves. Watch out for bruising on the top in the vice

Clean up the grooves with abrasive paper wrapped around a piece of scrap after the block is shaped

Disguise your next box of tissues with a mitred cover using contrasting wood

box, except of course at the final corner.

4 Dry assemble the box to check the joints. Mitre can be very tricky. Once satisfied use a strap cramp to glue up the four parts.

5 With the box in the strap cramp measure across the diagonals to check that it is square.

6 Plane up the material for the top facing and cut to length so that it fits

in the rebate. Round over the edges.

7 Fill the rebate at each end with a small fillet between the two facings. Then glue facings in place.

8 Screw retaining buttons in the bottom rebate.

CUTTING LIST

	LENGTH	WIDTH	THKNS
A End (2)	191mm	61mm	13mm
B Side (2)	343mm	61mm	13mm
C Top facing (2)	326mm	50mm	10mm

The tissue box cover needs to suit the size of the brand you buy. This design fits one of those 'man-size' boxes which are pretty standard.

HOW TO MAKE THE TISSUE BOX COVER

1 Start with the sides and ends of the box. Plane them to thickness and width but keep in one length if possible at this stage. You want to do as much of the machining as you can in one go.

2 Form a rebate along the top edge and another along the bottom edge of the sides and ends. These are for the turn-buttons and the top facings.

3 Use a mitre saw or mitre box to cut the 45° mitres at the corners. Try to arrange the joints in such a way that you have grain running around the

Details of the tissue box cover (all dimensions in mm)

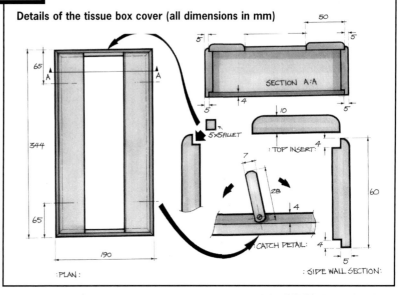

Use a mitre box or block to cut the joints for the side and ends. Mitres can be a pain, so take your time

Strap cramps are brilliant for assembling mitred components. Nylon straps do not stick to the glue

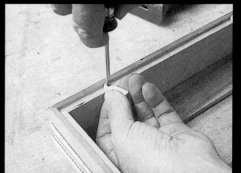

Finally screw little retaining buttons into the bottom rebate of the sides and ends to hold in the tissue box

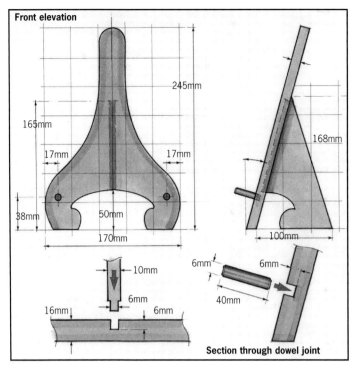

Front elevation

245mm
165mm
17mm 17mm
38mm
50mm
170mm

168mm
100mm

10mm
6mm
16mm   6mm

6mm   6mm
40mm

Section through dowel joint

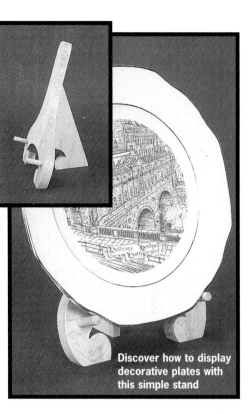

Discover how to display decorative plates with this simple stand

fence to cut the groove.

2 Now cut out the shape with a jigsaw, fretsaw or coping saw. Keep the cuts as smooth as possible so that you have the least cleaning up to do.

3 Clean up the curves by hand or use a foam drum sander powered by a drill. These are great for working on curved surfaces.

4 Cut out and shape the rear support. It is best to rebate both sides a little so that it slots into the groove. Make sure the rear support is a little longer than the groove so that you have a short shoulder at the top of the support.

5 Cut out the shape on the rear support, using the front foot as a guide and our drawings as a template. Now all you have to do is drill the holes for the little dowels that support the plate.

6 Clean up the plate rack with abrasive and then finish with varnish or oil.

It helps to have a router to make a stand, but it is not essential. You could cut the groove for the rear support by hand.

CUTTING LIST			
	LENGTH	WIDTH	THKNS
A Front foot (1)	245mm	170mm	16mm
B Support (1)	168mm	100mm	10mm
C Dowel (2)	40mm	8mm	8mm

HOW TO MAKE THE STAND

1 Cut out the front foot. This stand was made from solid maple, but you can use ply or MDG for painting. Draw out the shape, using our template as a guide. Before you cut out the shape work the groove on the back. You will find it very hard to hold the front foot down after it has been cut to shape. Use the router against a batten or with its

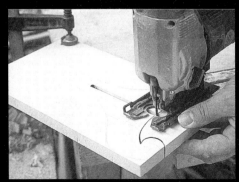

Use a jigsaw, fretsaw or coping saw to cut out the front of the plate rack. Keep close to the line to reduce cleaning up

Use a foam drum sander on a power drill to clean up the curves on the front of the plate rack

The bottom edge of the front and support are angled back a little. Do this on a disc sander, or with a plane

Make a holder for Sellotape or masking tape by laminating wood.

HOW TO MAKE THE DISPENSER

1 You can use any timber for making the dispenser, though contrasting types look best. Start by planning them smooth and cutting them roughly to shape. Make a card template first. Then cut away the semi-circular recess from the central lamination. You can do this roughly with a jigsaw, and then smooth it with a foam-filled abrasive drum. You will not be able to do this later.

2 Remember to cut a slot in this central piece (A) at this stage for the cutting bar. You can stick a blade in this slot, available from a good stationers.

3 Hold the three pieces together temporarily with cramps, and mark on the position for the L-shaped slot for the tape holder axle. It is important that these grooves line up, otherwise the tape is off-centre. You can easily chisel out this groove, but alternatively use a router, making a template for the router guide bush to follow. Clean up the grooves (in B) with a thin chisel and check the dowel fits.

4 Glue up the three pieces with PVA. Use a square to check that the grooves are lined up properly. The better the sides are lined up the less cleaning up you will need on the outside later.

MAKING THE HOLDER

5 While the glue sets you can make the triangular holder for the roll of tape.

Cut out a triangle of wood with sides just about 81mm long (C). This is not exact because you will now round over the ends to make it fit inside the roll.

6 Drill the centre of a piece of 6mm diameter dowel. It helps to angle the sides of the holder. That way the holder is tapered which makes it easier to push inside the roll. Otherwise it can be too tight or too loose.

7 Take the dispenser out of the cramps and sand it smooth with an abrasive flapwheel or a drum sander.

8 Cut the slot for the blade and plane the bottom of the dispenser so that it sits tidily on your desk.

9 Round over the edges of the dispenser and sand through the grades of abrasive, or for dense hardwoods like elm and maple, finish with wax. polish.

CUTTING LIST

	LENGTH	WIDTH	THKNS
A (1off, maple)	250mm	105mm	30mm
B (2 off, elm)	250mm	105mm	21mm
B (1 off, elm)	81mm	81mm	21mm

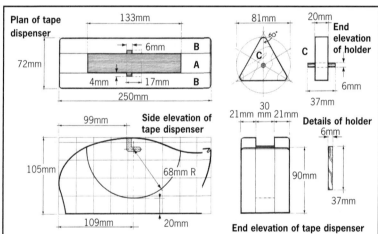

Plan of tape dispenser — 133mm — 6mm — B / A — 72mm — 4mm — 17mm — B — 250mm

Side elevation of tape dispenser — 99mm — 105mm — 68mm R — 109mm — 20mm

81mm — 60° — C — 20mm — End elevation of holder — C — 37mm — 6mm

30mm — 21mm mm 21mm — 90mm — 37mm — Details of holder — 6mm

End elevation of tape dispenser

Cut the recess for the tape out of the central lamination using a jigsaw or coping saw and then smooth it back with a foam filled abrasive drum

Cramp up the three pieces without glue to mark out the position for the L-shaped grooves into which the dowel supporting the triangular holder fits

The easiest way to hold a tape is on a triangular piece of wood. Round the ends of the triangle to fit. You can buy the inserts for cutting the tape

HOW TO MAKE THE TEA BAG TIDY

1 Plane a length of timber for the base and sides. Maple has been used here but you could use MDF and paint it. Before cutting the sides (A) to shape mark out the positions for the halving joints.

2 Cut the joints so that one pair of sides drop over the other two. The slots need to be good and tight as any gaps will show up.

3 Take the joints apart and cut the angled ends and the curve along the top edge. Cut the base to size and dry assemble the sides on the base. The sides will only need the smallest amount of PVA glue to fix to the base.

CUTTING LIST			
	LENGTH	WIDTH	THKNS
A Side (4)	134mm	64mm	5mm
B Base (1)	134mm	134mm	5mm

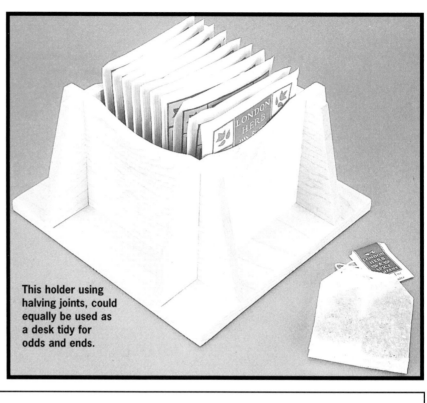

This holder using halving joints, could equally be used as a desk tidy for odds and ends.

Cut the halving joints with a tenon saw, or, if you have one, a radial arm saw. Assemble with a bit of glue. This joint must be pretty tight and self-supporting

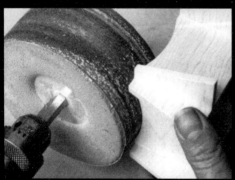

Before gluing the base to the sides, use a drum sander to shape the curves along the top edges. Cramp it between thick boards for gluing on the base

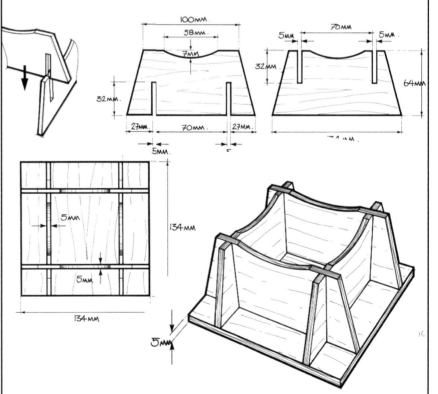

As CDs are often attractive packages they deserve display, and need easy access.

HOW TO MAKE THE CD RACK

1 Start by planing the sides (A) to thickness. If you are careful, by marking them out top to toe you ought to be able to cut both pieces from one piece only a little longer than each. You may get a better grain match for the sides if you do not cut them side by side. American walnut has been used for the sides and maple for the back (B) and shelves (C), but you could use any timbers. It is good to have contrast.

2 Rout the groove for the back, 6mm from the edge, with the sides overlength. Now you can plane the back (B) to the appropriate thickness to suit your router cutter. Then plane the back to width. Cut the sides to shape. The base is cut at 66° to the front edge. You can now dry assemble the back and sides.

Start by routing the groove in the sides for the back. Note the grain is parallel to the groove

If you have a radial arm saw that cuts the grooves well, but you could easily make a router jig

Do a dry run first to check the fit. This also gives you the angle for bevelling the top of the back

3 Rout the grooves for the CD shelves. A standard CD box is a fraction over 10mm thick. You can buy slimline and thicker boxes, but most are the standard size, which is over 142mm long and 125mm wide. The gap between the sides must be wide enough to take the width of the CDs. They must face forward so that you can read the spine.

4 If you are planning to make a few racks it is worth making a routing jig for the shelves. One way would be to fix a false base to the router. To this base is screwed a batten that slides in the shelf groove. Then all you have to do is rout the first groove, fix the false base to the router and use each groove as a guide for the next one. The batten must be a good fit, but not too tight.

5 Plane to thickness and cut to width and length. Note the grain must go from front to back. Chamfer the edges slightly. Assemble the rack using PVA adhesive, cramping up the sides and back first and then sticking in the shelves. These ought to be a push fit and need no cramping. Fit the shelves one at a time, cleaning away any excess glue as you go. It helps to do any finishing before assembling the rack as access will be limited.

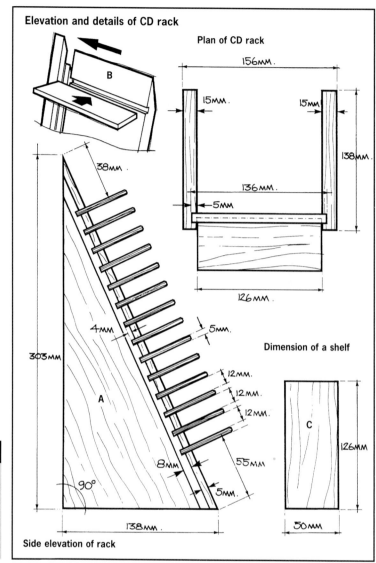

Elevation and details of CD rack

Plan of CD rack

156MM.

15MM   15MM

138MM

136MM

5MM

126MM.

38MM.

4MM   5MM

303MM

12MM.

12MM.

12MM.

A

8MM   55MM

90°   5MM

138MM.

Dimension of a shelf

C

126MM

50MM.

Side elevation of rack

CUTTING LIST			
	LENGTH	WIDTH	THKNS
A Side (2)	332mm	126mm	15mm
B Back (1)	321mm	131mm	8 mm
C Shelf (14)	52 mm	126mm	5mm

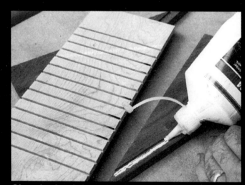
Glue the back into the sides with PVA. A couple of G-cramps for F-cramps will hold it together

Cut up the shelves, with the grain running from front to back. Chamfer the edges with a block plane

If you feel confident enough, cramp up all the shelves in one go with two cramps and scrapwood

a loose tongue, unless the tongue is hidden, like a biscuit.

5 If the tongue is open, make the sides of the jig shorter so that they do not interfere with the tongues. These are best left proud until the glue has set. Plane them flush, and chamfer the outer edges.

● ● ● ● ●
MATERIALS YOU WILL NEED

● **TOOLS – SAUCEPAN STAND**
Plane
Tenon saw
Chisel
Drill
Cramps
Biscuit jointer

● **TOOLS – KNIFE BLOCK**
Vice
Hand drill
Chisel
Smoothing plane
Tenon saw
Combination square
Router

● **MATERIALS**
1m (3ft) of 125 x ex25mm PAR

HOW TO MAKE A SAUCEPAN STAND

1 Plane up the three pieces preferably making full use of any offcuts you have.

2 Cut the ends at 30°. If you have a mitre saw then you will need to do very little marking out. Otherwise use a sliding bevel and square, and cut with a tenon saw. Make up your own mitre box with angles at 30°, for repetitive, accurate cuts.

3 For a stand held together with loose tongues, mark the grooves with a mortice gauge. Cut the cheeks with a tenon saw, and chop out the waste with a chisel. Making sure the grain does not break out, by chiselling inwards. It is important that the tongue fits tightly in the groove, with no gaps. Cut back the groove a fraction towards the centre so that the tongue fits right to the bottom of the groove where it can be seen on the outside edges of the stand.

4 Make a jig for cramping up the stand. This simply needs a base, to which are screwed three pieces. The apex of the stand fits neatly between two of these, while the third is about 19mm (3/4in) from the base to make room for two sets of folding wedges. These cramp up the stand. The jig is designed for a biscuited joint, and will not work so well for

		CUTTING LIST			
	MATERIAL	QTY	LENGTH	WIDTH	THKNS
L Side	Hardwood	3	257mm	50mm	15mm

Cutting lists always give the full length of a piece including the joint, but not wastage. Allow at least 25mm (1in) extra for length and 5mm on the width and thickness of sawn stock.

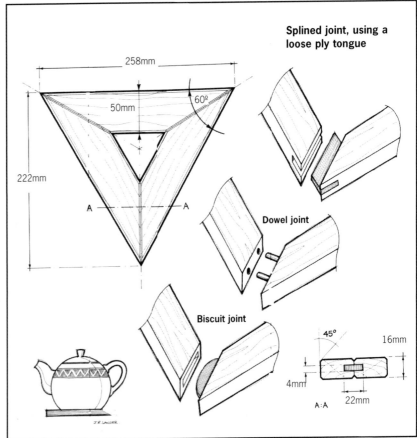

Splined joint, using a loose ply tongue

258mm

50mm

60°

222mm

A — A

Dowel joint

Biscuit joint

45°

16mm

4mm

22mm

A:A

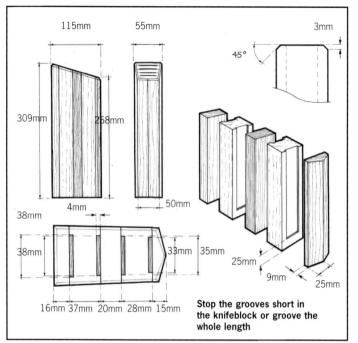

115mm   55mm   3mm
                          45°

309mm   258mm

            4mm   50mm
38mm

38mm   33mm 35mm
                 25mm
                9mm   25mm

16mm 37mm 20mm 28mm 15mm

Stop the grooves short in the knifeblock or groove the whole length

obvious tool for the job) you may find it easier to cut the shoulder with a handsaw, and take the groove the whole length of each piece. This will at least allow rubbish to fall through. Notice that the grooves get narrower towards the front, which is a design feature that reflects the tapering of the sides of the block.

This block is tapered or bevelled in a number of dimensions. But this is done after the strips are glued up.

HOW TO MAKE A KNIFEBLOCK

1 Plane your pieces to any thickness, but keep them the same width, if possible. Make sure the timber you select for the front is the best grain, and that it is thick enough for the bevelling. You will probably find it best to alternate between dark and light coloured timbers.

2 Cut a recess on both sides of two of the laminates, stopping the groove short of the bottom. If you are doing this by hand, without a router (the

3 Glue up the strips, making sure you keep glue away from the grooves. When the glue has set, cut the base off square and cut the top at an angle. Plane the bevels on the top at an angle. Plane the bevels on the front edge of the block and then taper the sides. Finally clean up and chamfer the top edges with a block plane.

	MATERIAL	QTY	LENGTH	WIDTH	THKNS
CUTTING LIST					
K Laminate	Hardwood	5	310mm	58mm	To suit

Rout out the groove on the laminates using a bench stop and batten to hold

Cramp up the laminates using PVA adhesive, and leave to set overnight

Having cut the angled top and tapered the side, chamfer the edges

63

HOW TO MAKE THE SHOE RACK

1 Decide on the number of shoes to be stored and allocate about 230mm (9in) running length of timber per pair. Prepare to size or buy planed timber measuring 260x152x19mm (10x6x¾in).

2 Make a template, draw a profile of the shoe on the timber, and shade the waste. Then cut the profile carefully to the line using a coping saw, jigsaw or bandsaw.

• • • • •

MATERIALS YOU WILL NEED

● **PAR PINE**
You need 2.54m of 150 x 19mm timber for the rack

• • • •

TOOLS YOU WILL NEED

● **ROUTER**
● **DRILL**
● **JIGSAW**
● **HAND TOOLS**

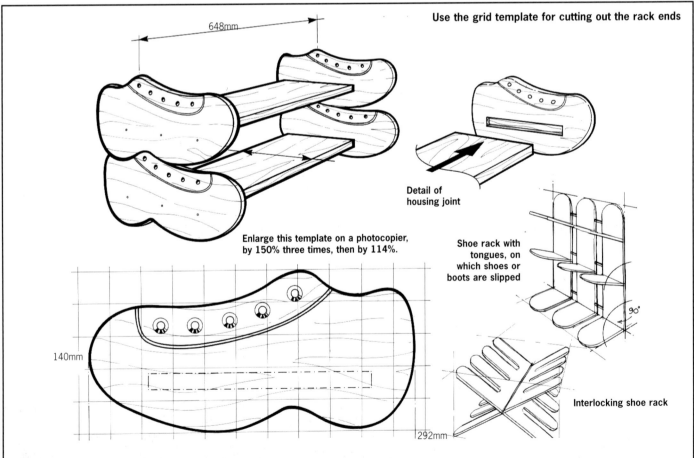

Use the grid template for cutting out the rack ends

648mm

Detail of housing joint

Enlarge this template on a photocopier, by 150% three times, then by 114%.

Shoe rack with tongues, on which shoes or boots are slipped

90°

140mm

292mm

Interlocking shoe rack

3 Now trim the profile accurately with a curved abrading stick or improvised former. Use the first shoe profile as the template for marking out the remaining shoe profiles on the wood. Number the shoe profiles according to how they will be linked to each other and fine-trim the contact surfaces ready for gluing.

4 Mark off the required lengths for the shoe supports and square a line round them. Using a tenon saw, jigsaw or bandsaw, cut the lengths off and trim the end-grain carefully with a smoothing plane or against a table disc sander.

5 Drill a 2mm (1/16in) hole at the centre line of the shoe supports on the shoe profile ends for easy location. Then drill the centres of the shoe support ends with the same pilot drill (for either pinning or screwing).

6 A fine V-groove, routed around the bridge of the shoe, is an attractive feature. First make an MDF template and use double-sided tape to fix it to the workpiece and the workpiece to the bench. Use a standard 18mm (3/4in) guide bush with the router. With a 6mm (1/4in) drill bit, carefully drill out the lace holes and countersink them on both sides.

7 Finishing off the components is done with a power sander or abrasive handblock for the flat surfaces and a curved abrading stick for the edges. This will give a rounded feel to the design.

8 Apply glue neatly to the ends of the supports and use pins to locate them through the pre-drilled holes in the ends. Hammer the pieces together at the appropriate angle and then drive in lost-head nails at either end, checking for precise alignment. Use a nailpunch - preferably a large one - with its tip ground flat, to sink in the pins. Then tidy up with wood filler.

9 Finally add a protective coating to your shoe rack by applying a colour-stained polyurethane and varnish with a brush.

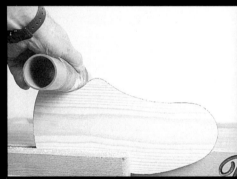
Use a template to mark out the ends, cut them to shape with a jigsaw and sand the edges with a block

Drill a 2mm pilot hole along the centre line of the shoe shelf on the profiles for easy location

Fix a wooden template to the profile for routing the details, cut smaller than the shape

Drill out the lace holes with a 6mm bit, and countersink from both sides of each end piece

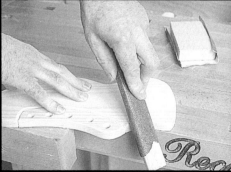
Use an abrasive stick for rounding over all the edges, having sanded the flat surfaces with a power sander

For gluing tiered ends together use PVA and double-sided tape. The tape holds them while the glue sets

4 Remove the wood from the drill, and sand the inside of the hole with a flapwheel sanding attachment in an electric drill. Go carefully with the flapwheel as it can burn the wood.

5 Mark out a 50mm (2in) square around the hole, or hexagonal angles to make it different. Cut out the square shape from the piece of wood using a bandsaw and cut off the corners as marked.

6 Sand each cut side, and the top and bottom, with a sanding disc until smooth and finish off by hand with fine abrasive paper. You can make a lathe into a sanding disc by fitting a platform to the bed. Stain, polish or paint as desired.

7 This will produce a hexagonal ring but the outer shape can be any shape you choose.

HOW TO MAKE NAPKIN RINGS USING A PILLAR DRILL

1 Take a piece of hardwood thicknessed to about 25mm (1in).

2 Clamp your wood onto the pillar drill table using strong G-cramps, with a piece of 18mm (¾in) thick scrap MDF underneath. Mark the centre with a punch to guide the drill bit.

3 Fit a spade bit, sawtooth bit or a standard or an adjustable Forstner bit (set to 40mm (1⁹⁄₁₆in) in the pillar drill), and drill right down through the wood into the scrap MDF. Make sure the depth stop is set to stop you hitting the metal table. It is worth making a note on the drill to do so!

Use an adjustable bit for drilling out the centre of napkin rings. Set the bit to 40mm. Cramp down the wood.

Use a flapwheel in a power drill for cleaning up the internal surfaces. Be careful as you go as flapwheels can burn the wood if used too hard.

Mark out the exterior shape of the napkin ring after you have drilled the hole. You can make the outside to any shape you want.

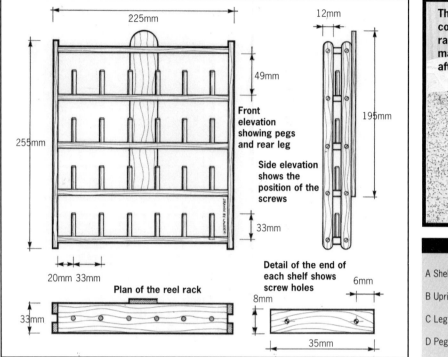

225mm

12mm

49mm

Front elevation showing pegs and rear leg

195mm

255mm

Side elevation shows the position of the screws

33mm

20mm 33mm

Plan of the reel rack

33mm

Detail of the end of each shelf shows screw holes

6mm

8mm

35mm

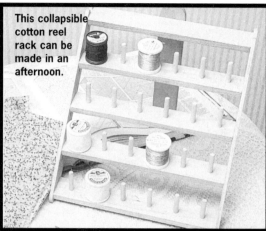

This collapsible cotton reel rack can be made in an afternoon.

	MATERIAL	QTY	LENGTH	WIDTH	THKNS
A Shelf	Hardwood	5	215mm	35mm	8mm
B Upright	Hardwood	4	250mm	12.5mm	6mm
C Leg	Hardwood	1	200mm	35mm	6mm
D Peg	Dowel	24	33mm		6mm

CUTTING LIST

HOW TO MAKE YOUR RACK

1 Mark out the prepared timber accurately and drill four of the five shelves to accept the dowel pins. The holes must be evenly spaced and just big enough for the dowel to fit in them tightly. Test the fit by drilling a piece of scrap wood first.

If you have a vertical drill stand, use the depth stop to make sure that all the holes are drilled to the same depth. Alternatively, use a piece of masking tape wrapped round the drill bit as a depth guide. But you must hold the drill perpendicular to the wood. Mark out the ends of the shelves and to drill pilot holes for the screws at this stage.

2 Drill a 3mm (⅛in) hole for No 4 screws, using masking tape to hold the uprights together while drilling. Each hole in the uprights must be countersunk and form only a slack fit with the shank of the screw. Round off the ends of the uprights either by using a sanding disk or by chiselling off the corners and finishing with glasspaper.

3 Cut all the dowel pegs to the same length.

4 Glue in the dowel pegs with PVA adhesive, making sure that they are all in line (check alignment by looking along from the end of the shelf).

5 Fix the uprights to the shelves, using a steel screw first to make a path for the brass screws. Screw the rear leg to the top shelf. Finish with Colron wax, or polyurethane.

To get all the holes for the dowels use a drill stand. Alternatively use a piece of masking tape as a depth stop

Make a V-jig to cut the dowel pegs to length on a bandsaw. Considering you have 24 to cut it is worth the effort

Finally screw and glue the rear leg in position. This must be firm as it will be used as the handle to open the rack

The strips under bookends ensure that these stay in place, while the shape of bookends puts them in context with any literary taste. Try to pick timber so the spine of each bookend is free of knots.

● ● ● ● ● ●
MATERIALS YOU WILL NEED

● **MATERIALS**
  18x4x2in sawn
  softwood
  Bottle of turps
  Polyurethane
  Brush
  8 x No. 6 CSK screws
  Two 220 flour papers
  1m of 100mm 100 grit

● **TOOLS**
  Vice
  Hand drill
  Chisel
  Smoothing plane
  Tenon saw
  square

View of bookend from above and below

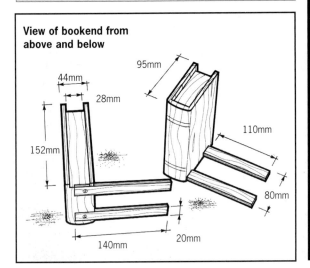

MAKING A PAIR OF BOOKENDS IN EIGHT EASY STEPS

You'll need a 460mm (18in) piece of 50x100mm (2x4in) sawn pine which is cheaper than PAR, and can be planed to size

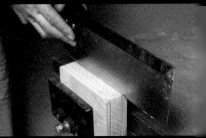

Having cut the workpiece into two bookends and one piece for the strips, mark out the grooves and cut the shoulders

As far as you can, cut the shoulders on the end-grain then remove waste with chisel and hammer (mallet preferred)

Clean up the stopped shoulder on the groove by paring back to the line gradually, holding the chisel upright

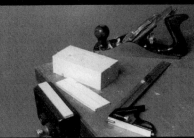

Cut thin slivers off the extra piece left over, then cut these in half to produce the strips and plane smooth

Use the end of the combination square to mark out the recesses for the strips underneath the bookends

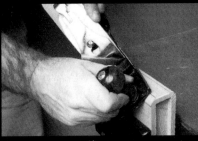

Mark lines 6mm (¼in) in from each edge of the spine and then plane the radius. Using a block plane may be easier

Mark each housing for each strip and, with them fitted firmly, drill a clearance hole and a pilot hole for screws.

HOW TO MAKE THE NIGHT LIGHT HOLDER

1 Select and prepare a piece of hardwood. Decide on the number of candles and divide the top side into squares. Mark diagonals for drill centres.

2 Saw the block off to length using either a tenon saw or a bandsaw.

3 Select the matching flat bit for your candle diameter and drill blind holes for the candles using a power drill (preferably bench-mounted to get it right). The night lights used required a 38mm (1½in) bit. If you have one, a Forstner, or shark's tooth is best for drilling out candle holes. However, if you only have a flat bit, touch it up with an oilstone and it will serve you well. Make sure the hole is just so deep that you can pull out the night light. The depth is set at 25mm (1in), with the candles protruding by about 2mm (1/16in).

4 Using a domestic plate or similarly curved object, mark out the profile of the candle holder. Be sure to keep within the guidelines of the original squares.

5 After shading the waste, use a bandsaw (fitted with a fresh blade) to cut the curves carefully to the line. If you don't have a bandsaw, you can use a jigsaw or coping saw instead. On some curves you will have to feed the blade in with no excess to one side. Work carefully with a sharpened blade.

6 Use a bandsaw (or a tenon saw) to texture the outer edges by just kissing the surface with the blade. Cuts approximately 2mm (1/8in) deep are made 2mm apart. This can be guessed or marked off with a pencil. Take care to keep your hands well away from the blade, and make sure you space these cuts evenly so they flow around the surface.

7 All the top surface needs is a series of very fine drill holes to denote the contour of each shape and give the impression of three blocks stuck together. The holes do not even need to be very deep, but do watch out that the drill bit does not wander on such a small scale. It is worth marking each hole with a bradawl first.

8 Finally sand the smooth surfaces of the candle holder and soften over all edges with medium grit abrasive, wrapped around a wooden or cork block.

9 Apply two coats of matt polyurethane varnish, leaving six hours between coats. Baize can be stuck to the base if required.

This stylish design for a candle holder will add a little romance at the dinner table.

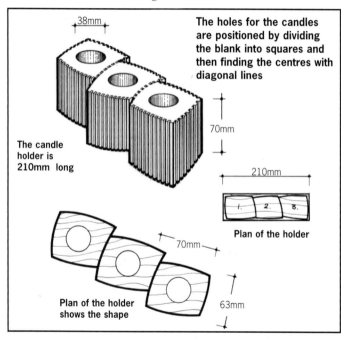

The holes for the candles are positioned by dividing the blank into squares and then finding the centres with diagonal lines

38mm

70mm

The candle holder is 210mm long

210mm

Plan of the holder

70mm

Plan of the holder shows the shape

63mm

Having marked the centres for the holes with diagonals, drill out using the flat bit keeping the drill vertical

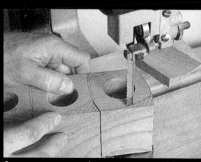

As you cut away the waste you will begin to get a feel of the candle holder and the shape you are creating

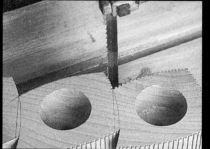

Keep the texture even around the candle holder so that it looks consistent and feels smooth

You could make the interlocking trays from any wood.

4 Cut the pieces for the sides and back to 333mm and 238mm respectively. Next cut the mitres on the ends.

5 Now prepare the base from MDF or ply, and rebate to produce a tongue to go into the groove. Also prepare the stock for the front strip that joins the sides. As with the sides and back, cut a groove for the base using a router.

6 Dry assemble the box without glue to check the joints. If you are satisfied, glue the base into the groove and glue up the mitres.

7 Once the glue has set clean up the joints and make a 6mm-thick top to catch dust.

CUTTING LIST			
	LENGTH	WIDTH	THKNS
A Side	333mm	46mm	9mm
B Back	238mm	46mm	9mm
C Front	238mm	17mm	9mm
D Base	324mm	229mm	4mm

HOW TO MAKE THE TRAYS

1 Start by planing the material for the sides and back to 46 x 9mm. Do not cut the sides and end to length until you have routed the groove for the base.

2 Use a router to cut the groove in the 46x9mm boards. The groove needs to be 4.5mm deep and 5mm wide, though its width depends on what you are using for the base. Also cut the rebates on the top and bottom edges for the trays to interlock. Do not mould the top edge until you have cut the curves.

3 Make yourself a template of the radius for the end of the sides. There is one concave radius and one convex, but they are both 14.5mm radius. Cut the radius with a bandsaw or jigsaw, and sand them smooth with a drum sander.

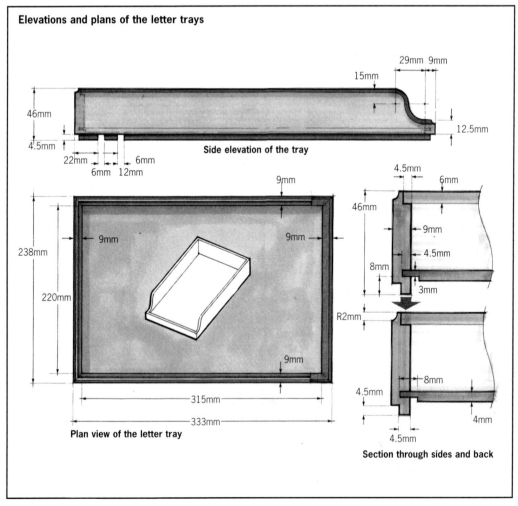

Elevations and plans of the letter trays

Side elevation of the tray

Plan view of the letter tray

Section through sides and back

You can make them easily from a small offcut of elm, teak or choice pine, cutting the shape with a bandsaw and finishing with a spokeshave and various grades of abrasive.

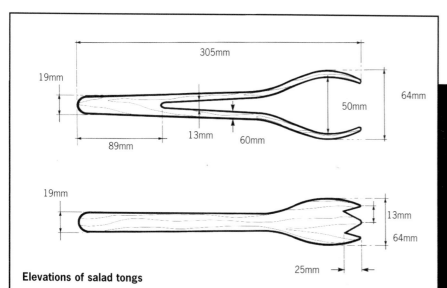

Elevations of salad tongs

305mm
19mm
64mm
50mm
13mm
60mm
89mm

19mm
13mm
64mm
25mm

HOW TO MAKE SALAD TONGS

1 Start by drawing out a fork shape on your block of wood, and then shade the waste to be cut away

2 Cut around the shape on a bandsaw, noting that accuracy reduces cleaning up later

3 Cut across the tips and then down the teeth, keeping your fingers clear; butchers also use the bandsaws!

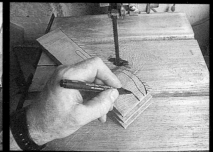

4 You can either draw the profile freehand or glue on a paper template, before cutting to shape

5 Use the waste from the first cut as a template for the second cut. Cut the inside nudging round the radius

6 Use the end of the combination square to mark out the recesses for the strips underneath the bookends

7 Use 60grit abrasive paper around a stell rule to produce the final shape, and for finishing the inside

Try a bit of carving to make this stylish cake slice

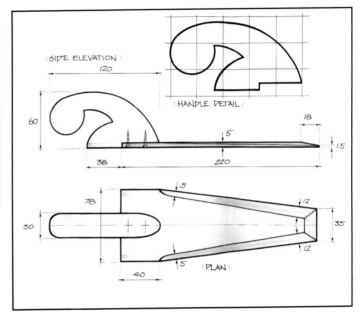

: SIDE ELEVATION :
120
: HANDLE DETAIL :
60
38
220
18
5
15
78
30
5
12
35
12
40
5
: PLAN :

You may choose to use beech because it is close-grained, for strength in the blade. It's also quite easy to carve, though you may prefer something softer like lime for the handle and experiment with contrasting handle and blade.

HOW TO MAKE THE CAKE SLICE

1 Start with the handle and then make the blade to fit. The first thing to do is draw out roughly the shape of the handle. You can do this directly onto the wood or make a card template.

2 It helps greatly if you have a bandsaw for cutting out the handle shape. However for a small job like this you can use a coping saw, or a jigsaw.

3 Hold the handle in a vice for carving.

4 Remove the corners and as much of the waste as possible with a chisel. Then use any rasps or files you have to hand to round over the corners and make the handle more comfortable.

5 Once you are satisfied with the shape use abrasive to smooth the handle.

6 Now plane up the blade and cut to shape. How you shape the blade depends on what you hope it to cut. You may want it shorter and fatter, for instance.

7 With a block plane bevel the top of the blade. The bevel needs to be as long as possible at the tip to make the blade sharp, but try not to lose any strength along the leading edge.

8 Cut a notch out of the bottom of the handle, at the front to take the blade.

You might prefer to do this before carving when the sides of the handle are still square.

9 Screw the blade up into the handle, making sure the screwheads are well below the surface. You can leave the wood unfinished for cakes.

CUTTING LIST

	LENGTH	WIDTH	THKNS
A Handle (1)	125mm	65mm	30mm
B Blade (1)	220mm	77mm	5mm

Draw the shape of the handle onto the wood (freehand or with a template) and then cut out the shape roughly

Remove the bulk of the waste with a chisel, naturally working away from yourself all the time for safety's sake

Screw the blade to the handle with brass screws making sure the screw heads are below the surface of the blade

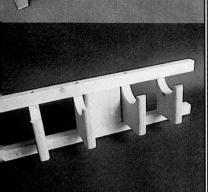

■ CHAPTER 4 ■

FURNITURE

How to tidy up all those hats and coats and furnish the hall with a shelf.

HOW TO MAKE THE SHELF

1 If possible, buy all the timber from the same stock so that the grain and colour are consistent. Pine sold planed all round (PAR) is fine, but if you intend to glue two or more together to make the shelf and back plate, do not rely on the edges being square. Equally once you have planed the edges straight and square, do not leave the pieces lying around before gluing up as they will probably move and no long fit together exactly. If you do not have sash cramps, make a cramping jig, with a chipboard base to which are screwed two parallel battens. Place the boards to be glued between the battens, and use folding wedges to tighten.

2 Cut both the back plate and shelf to length, with the shelf a little bit longer than the back. This is for visual effect, to draw the eye towards the shelf.

3 Shape two corners on both boards. To round the corners first draw a guide line using the edge of a jar, tin or with a compass. Cut off the corner with a jigsaw or coping saw, keeping to the waste side of the line. Tidy up the corner with a spokeshave and then glasspaper. Repeat on the other corners.

4 With the corners shaped and sanded smooth, hold each board down on the workbench and run a router along the front edge of the shelf and the bottom edge of the back plate. This is naturally best done with a bearing guided cutter, working from the underside so that the bearing runs along the uncut top edge.

If you have neither a router nor moulding planes, this moulding will be difficult to produce, so you may want to round over or bevel the edge with a smoothing plane or block plane.

5 When it comes to shaping the supports it is easiest to draw the profile by eye. Having cut the first support, transfer the outline on to the second one. To finish the supports, secure them both in a vice with the edges flush and run a sanding wheel over them, then finish with glasspaper by hand.

6 To mount the supports, take the back plate and measure 51mm (2in) from each edge. Mark two parallel lines to show the position of the support bracket. Mark the centre of these two lines and drill two through holes. Hold the back in a vice, and offer the

Boards are less likely to bow with sash cramps above and below. If there is any bowing use wedges under the top two cramps

Having marked the rounded corner from a suitable jam jar, cut the curve with a jigsaw. If you do not have such a tool, use a coping saw

Use the curve of one bracket to mark the profile on the other.
The edges of the timber must have been planed square and straight first

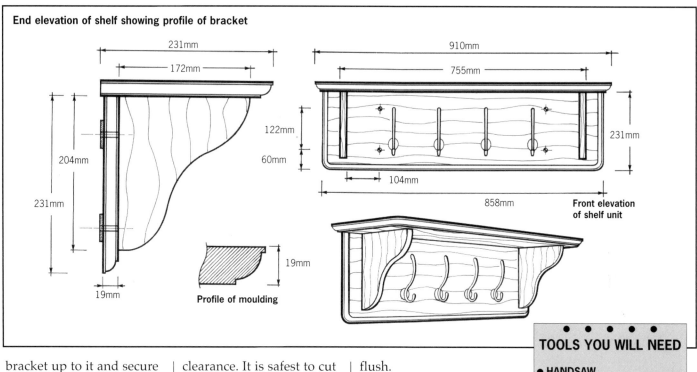

End elevation of shelf showing profile of bracket

231mm

172mm

204mm

231mm

19mm

19mm

Profile of moulding

910mm

755mm

122mm

60mm

104mm

858mm

231mm

Front elevation of shelf unit

bracket up to it and secure with a screw. Repeat with the other bracket.

7 Now all you have to do is fix the shelf and hooks. From the positions of the brackets, mark where to drill screw holes on the top of the shelf. Drill shallow holes to suit your plug cutter, and then all the way through the shelf for screw clearance. It is safest to cut the plug holes with brace and bit, or flat bit in the power drill, which will not pull through the wood.

8 Make four plugs from an offcut, and with some glue in each hole tap them into position. When the glue is dry, take off the protruding end of the plug with a sharp chisel and sand flush.

9 With an oak stain on the finished shelf and some attractive brass hooks, it is ready for fixing.

TOOLS YOU WILL NEED

- HANDSAW
- DRILL OR BRACE ● AND BIT
- ROUTER
- JIGSAW OR COPING SAW
- SASH CRAMPS
- CHISEL

CUTTING LIST					
	MATERIAL	QTY	LENGTH	WIDTH	THKNS
A Shelf	Pine	1	910mm	231mm	19mm
B Back plate	Pine	1	858mm	231mm	19mm
C Bracket	Pine	2	204mm	172mm	19mm

Mark the position of the brackets on the back plate and drill clearance holes for fixing the brackets. You may want to cut a housing instead

Mark the positions for the brackets on the shelf once they have been screwed to the back plate. It helps to continue these lines across the top as well

Screw the shelf to the brackets having drilled pilot holes in the brackets. This is important when screwing into end-grain which may split

75

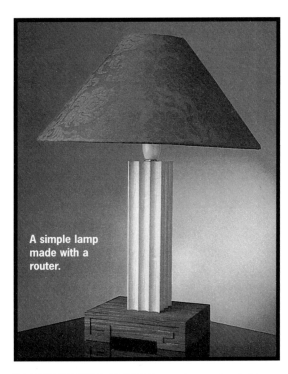

A simple lamp made with a router.

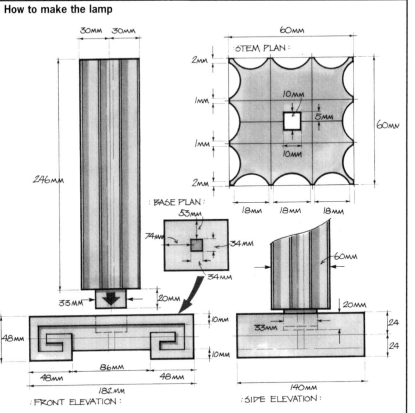

30MM 30MM

246MM

33MM

48MM

48MM 86MM 48MM

182MM

: FRONT ELEVATION :

STEM PLAN

2MM
1MM
1MM
2MM

60MM

10MM
5MM
10MM

60MM

18MM 18MM 18MM

: BASE PLAN :

53MM
74MM
34MM
34MM

20MM

10MM
10MM

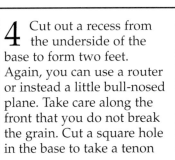

60MM

20MM

33MM

24
24

140MM

: SIDE ELEVATION :

MAKING THE FLUTED LAMP

1 For a table lamp you need a hole down the core to take the cable. The quickest way to do this is to glue two pieces of wood together with a groove down the centre.

2 Once the glue has set, plane the upright square and then rout the flutes with a radius cutter in a router table.

3 Glue up the wood for the base, unless you have a thick enough piece already. Mark out the decoration along the front edge. If you feel brave enough, you can use a router to remove the bulk of the waste and then clean up the decoration with a chisel by hand.

4 Cut out a recess from the underside of the base to form two feet. Again, you can use a router or instead a little bull-nosed plane. Take care along the front that you do not break the grain. Cut a square hole in the base to take a tenon on the upright. Make sure you cut the tenon on the upright before you work the fluting as the edges are thin and can easily be damaged. Drill the base for the cable, then fit the lamp attachment to the top.

Glue up the upright from the two pieces. This allows you to groove each piece first so that the cable can be fitted down the core

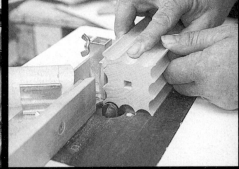

Use a radius cutter in a router table to flute the upright. Preferably use the feather boards to hold the work to the fence

Cut a square hole in the centre of the base, having cut a tenon on the end of the upright already

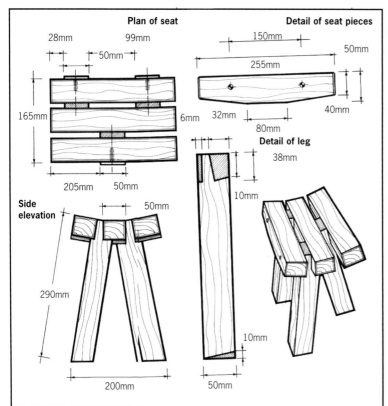

Plan of seat

28mm 99mm
50mm
165mm
6mm
205mm 50mm

Side elevation
50mm
290mm
200mm

Detail of seat pieces
150mm
50mm
255mm
32mm
80mm
40mm

Detail of leg
38mm
10mm
10mm
50mm

HOW TO MAKE A THREE-LEGGED STOOL

1 Select a length of knot and split free 50x50mm (2x2in) timber and square to size. Measure and mark lines. Saw to the appropriate lengths. Using a steel rule, try square, marking gauge and a pencil or ballpoint, mark out one top and one leg piece from which the others can be copied. Shade off the waste.

Saw and plane the tapers on the three top pieces which will form the seat. It helps to tilt the wood in the vice, so the sawing action is always vertical.

2 Saw the leg cutouts on the waste side of the lines you have marked. Place the wood in the vice horizontally and cut the shoulder lines using a tenon saw. Clean up any burrs on the inside of the joint with a sharp chisel.

3 Mark in 25mm (1in) on one top piece, drill and screw two legs in position. Use 38mm (1½in) No 10 CSK screws, drill pilot and shank holes first, then countersink so that the screw head lies under the surface.

4 Drill and screw the third leg centrally on the other side of the central top piece. Apply pressure at the shoulder line, as you drill to maintain a tight fit.

5 As the leg ends are protruding slightly, they will need to be marked flush to the top piece edge, ready to be sawn flush.

6 As the leg ends have been initially cut square, they will need cutting to the correct, compound angle.

7 Dismantle the legs, mount in the vice and then saw both ends to length.

8 Clean up all components with a smoothing plane and abrasive paper, removing all the preparation marks. Plane a bevel on all edges to soften the corners.

9 Apply glue to the leg assembly and use the screws as clamps. Then screw and glue the outer top pieces into position, angling the drill to just below the inner screws. Counterbore the holes, for short screws and tidiness.

10 After the stool has been glued and allowed to dry for at least eight hours, apply a few coats of lacquer for protection and to bring out the grain.

Mark out the joint at the top of one leg to act as a template for the rest

When taper planing, angle the wood so that the plane is horizontal

Likewise angle the leg to keep the saw vertical, making the cut easier

Having screwed the front two legs to the centre bar, fix on the back leg

HOW TO MAKE THE CUSHION

1 Cut thin strips of contrasting timber. The strips can all be the same thickness or all different. If you have an accurate sawbench, with a fine blade, you may be able to glue up the laminations directly from the saw, but you are better off planing the strips smooth. Make sure the sides are parallel to ensure the strips join up accurately at the corner.. The idea is to rest a carved wooden egg on the cushion.

2 For a square cushion 102mm (4in) wide, you really only need a laminated board 203mm (8in) long. But it is safer to glue up strips nearer 229mm (9in) long. Once dry, cut into four 50mm (2in) long pieces and then take off two corners to produce a triangle, 50mm (2in) high. Cut four triangles, and then flip two over, and glue them up in pairs to start. If the joints are not perfect you can plane the edge straight and square once the PVA adhesive has dried, and then join the halves together.

3 A bandsaw, if you have one, is the quickest way to round the edges of the cushion blank, having planed the base flat. Draw

Round off the corners of the cushion blank after the edges, noting the pull-up effect that a weight on a cushion has

Mark an area to be hollowed out for the egg in the centre, and use a spiralling action with a gouge, working out from the centre

With the hollow finished, move to the edges softening the curves and working inwards but leaving a high ground

Before you round the top of the cushion too far, mark a line to show the highest point, a couple of inches from the centre

Undercut the edges. When the sides are shaped roughly, the top of the flat area becomes a good guide for the edge seam

Soften the edges of the folds with a bent gouge on its back. Note how the seam runs a wavy path along the edge

out the profile before bandsawing, remembering that the edges of a cushion are pulled up by the weight of the egg.

4 Holding the cushion firmly for carving is essential, and gluing it to a base with a paper gasket is probably sufficient.

You can then cramp the board to the bench. The trouble with screwing the cushion to a board is that the screw holes will be visible later.

5 Carve out the hollow for the egg first to set the depth, use a 12mm (½in) No. 7 straight gouge for this, with a spiral action.

This is the same process you would use for hollowing out a bowl, starting in the centre and working out. Do not go too deep as the egg will not make much of an impression. You must start to consider the relationship between the size of the dent and the pull-up of the edges, and of the corners.

6 Having carved the hollow, start to round over the edges. Draw a sight line around the edges to show the mid-point, and work inwards gradually. The mid-point will be a touch higher than the centre line to account for pull-up. Leave a high area about 38mm (1½in) around the centre, and work towards it to blend the edges and dent. To ensure you do not cut back the softer areas you

may find it easiest to carve across the laminations.

7 With the top well smoothed, start undercutting the edges and rounding over the corners. Leave enough wood around the dent for details and definition, but develop a lump on each of the sides to give the impression of the corners being turned up.

8 Having carved the basic shape you can start to work in the details. Use a V-tool for this, first along the edges for a seam and then scattered around the cushion. Mark the seam as you round away the flats on the sides. You will find that the top line of the flat area is a good guide for the seam line, curving up and down. You can curve out a thin V

along the quarter lines, as patchwork is often sewn up in that way.

9 Smooth the details by turning a shallow gouge on its back and gently cutting away the fine edges of each V-line. Keep the details as random, as you'd expect on a patchwork cushion.

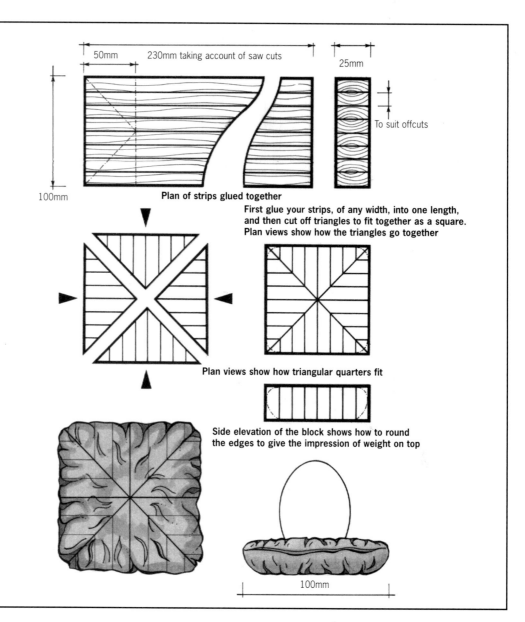

50mm 230mm taking account of saw cuts 25mm

100mm

To suit offcuts

Plan of strips glued together

First glue your strips, of any width, into one length, and then cut off triangles to fit together as a square. Plan views show how the triangles go together

Plan views show how triangular quarters fit

Side elevation of the block shows how to round the edges to give the impression of weight on top

100mm

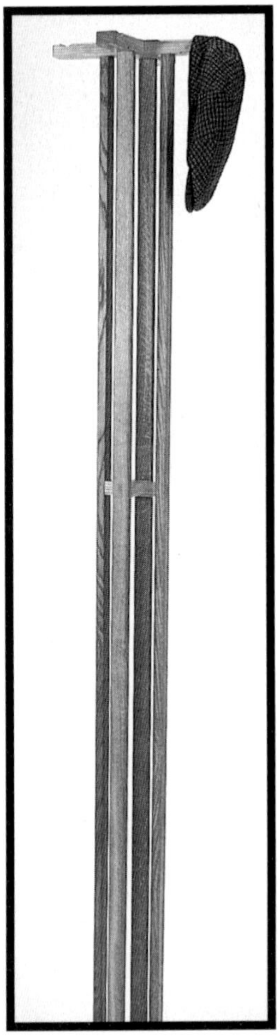

An understated stand which ought to suit any hall. Its construction is simple, using two types of joint. The feet (D), top pieces (B) and the dividers (C) are each assembled with cross-halving joints.

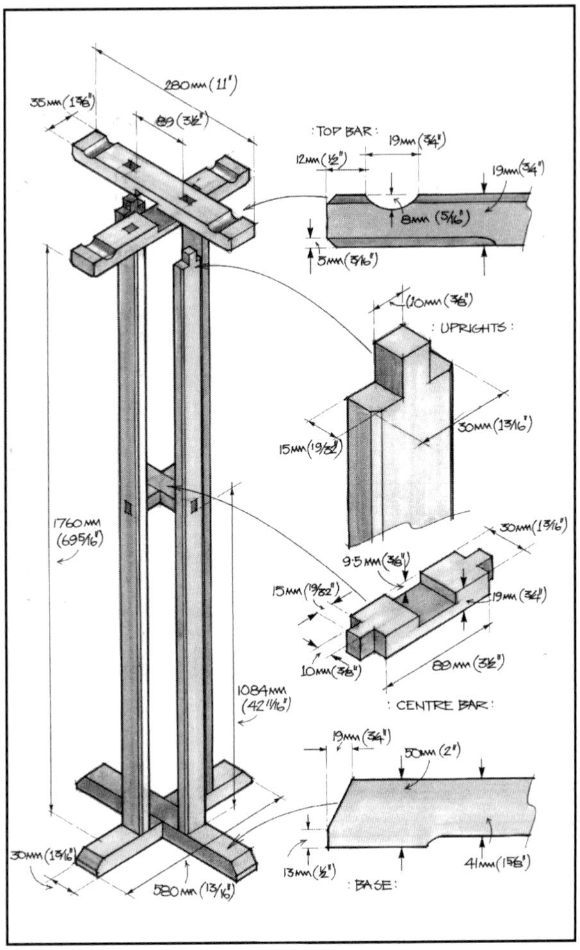
280mm (11")
35mm (1⅜")
89 (3½")
: TOP BAR :
19mm (¾")
12mm (½")
19mm (¾")
8mm (5/16")
5mm (3/16")
10mm (⅜")
: UPRIGHTS :
15mm (19/32")
30mm (1 3/16")
1760mm (69 5/16")
30mm (1 3/16")
9.5mm (⅜")
15mm (19/32")
19mm (¾")
10mm (⅜")
89mm (3½")
1084mm (42 11/16")
: CENTRE BAR :
19mm (¾")
50mm (2")
30mm (1 3/16")
580mm (13/16")
13mm (½")
: BASE :
41mm (1⅝")

The four uprights are tenoned into the feet and top, while the dividers are tenoned into the uprights. You could hang umbrellas off the little dividers if you want.

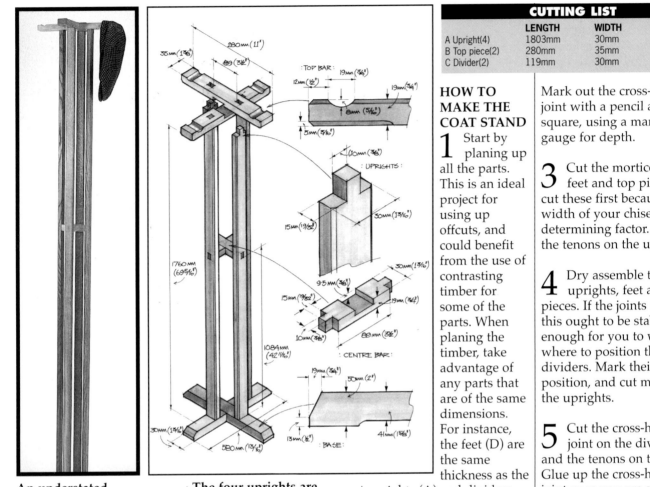

CUTTING LIST

	LENGTH	WIDTH	THKNS
A Upright(4)	1803mm	30mm	15mm
B Top piece(2)	280mm	35mm	19mm
C Divider(2)	119mm	30mm	19mm

HOW TO MAKE THE COAT STAND

1 Start by planing up all the parts. This is an ideal project for using up offcuts, and could benefit from the use of contrasting timber for some of the parts. When planing the timber, take advantage of any parts that are of the same dimensions. For instance, the feet (D) are the same thickness as the uprights (A) and dividers (C) are wide, so thickness them all at the same time.

2 Cut the feet and top pieces to length and roughly shape them.

Mark out the cross-halving joint with a pencil and square, using a marking gauge for depth.

3 Cut the mortices in the feet and top pieces. You cut these first because the width of your chisel is the determining factor. Then cut the tenons on the uprights.

4 Dry assemble the uprights, feet and top pieces. If the joints are good this ought to be stable enough for you to work out where to position the dividers. Mark their position, and cut mortices in the uprights.

5 Cut the cross-halving joint on the dividers, and the tenons on the ends. Glue up the cross-halving joint once you are satisfied with the fit. Then chamfer the uprights, feet and top.

6 Assemble the piece, having cut the hooks on the top pieces, and then finish.

Having planed the parts, cut the cross-halving joints and the mortices for the uprights on the feet

Now cut the cross-halving joints and the tenons on the short dividers that keep the uprights straight

To produce a 'hook' on which to hang coats, use a drum sander in a drillstand, with a fence and stop

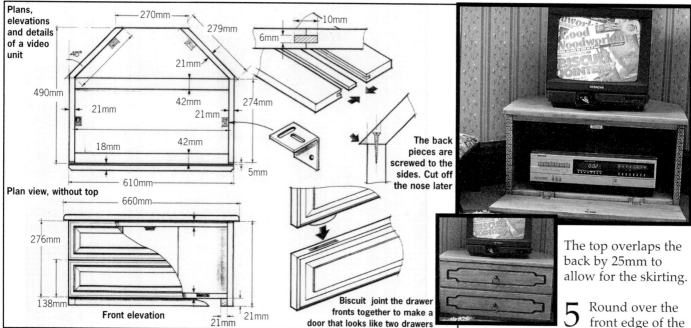

Plans, elevations and details of a video unit

270mm
279mm
45°
10mm
6mm
21mm
490mm
21mm
42mm
274mm
21mm
18mm
42mm
5mm
610mm

The back pieces are screwed to the sides. Cut off the nose later

Plan view, without top

660mm
276mm
138mm
Front elevation
21mm
21mm

Biscuit joint the drawer fronts together to make a door that looks like two drawers

The top overlaps the back by 25mm to allow for the skirting.

How to make a simple cupboard to hold a video and support a television.

HOW TO MAKE THE VIDEO UNIT

1 Construction begins with the base (A). Glue 100mm wide boards together to form a panel for the base. Once set, cut out the final shape from that panel.
Mark and measure carefully to ensure the base is symmetrical. If you are a unsure, then make a full-size template first from which you can cut.

2 Cut wood for the sides (B), cutting an angle of 67.5° down the rear vertical edge. You may have to do this before edge jointing the panels for the sides and back, because a mitre saw may not have the depth of cut. Make up the back pieces (C) next, with the same 67.5° angle on the edge. Mark the panels left and right, and screw the back to the side, then screw those to the base with supporting battens. Extend the holes in the battens (D) into slots to allow for movement.

4 Attach the front (H) to the base with cranked hinges, using magnetic catches at the top. Now make up the top panel (G) from four strips 100mm wide and one strip 120mm wide.

5 Round over the front edge of the top, and fix the top with expansion brackets. Add casters if you want the unit to move, and sand it all smooth, with the grain. Fix fake drawer handles to the front of the piece and lead cables through the back.

CUTTING LIST			
	LENGTH	WIDTH	THKNS
A Base(1)	569mm	490mm	21mm
B Side(2)	274mm	306mm	21mm
C Back(2)	279mm	306mm	21mm
D Batten(2)	274mm	21mm	21mm
E Fascia(1)	569mm	21mm	21mm
F Top front rail(1)	569mm	21mm	21mm
G Top(1)	660mm	520mm	21mm
H Front(1)	610mm	306mm	21mm

You can buy drawer fronts ready-made. These are then biscuit jointed (or dowelled) along one edge to produce a front that looks like drawers

The top, base, side and back panels are edge jointed. Make sure they do not bow in the cramps. Alternate the growth rings in the end-grain to stop cupping

Make a prototype mock-up to work out the angles at the back. A good tip is to add an extra rail at the join between the back and the sides for support

What makes this simple-to-make extendible shaving mirror possible is the use of rivets to hold the concertina-like arm together.

HOW TO MAKE THE SHAVING MIRROR

1 Start by making the mirror frame. This is rebated, twice, for the glass and ply back (C). Mitre the corners and assemble with a strap cramp or similar. The frame, and most of the other parts, are planed to 15mm thick so do all the planing in one go.

2 Now move to the back assembly that you screw to the wall. This is simply a back (M), a shelf

The mirror frame has a double rebate to take the mirror and the ply back. Screw the dowel support (K) to the ply back before fitting the back to the frame

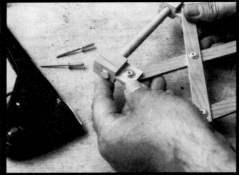

Once you have assembled the extendible arm, rivet the last slats to the lugs and fit them on the dowel. One lug must slide, but glue the other in place

Drill the base and shelf for a dowel and then screw and plug them to the back with the arm in place. Chamfer all the edges for a cleaner effect

(D) on the top
and a base (E)
below. Screw and
plug the shelf
and base to the
back. Do not
assemble until
you are ready to
include the rear
dowel upright
(H) and lugs (G).

3 The
extendible
arm (F) is made
from six thin
slats. You
assemble these in
a criss-cross
pattern, with the
four ends joined
to lugs that are
held on the
dowel uprights.
One lug at each
end must be able
to slide so that
the arm can
extend.

4 Start making
the arm by
drilling each slat
at the ends and
centre. Assemble
with rivets and
add the lugs. Note that the
tongue on each lug is offset
to account for the arm slats

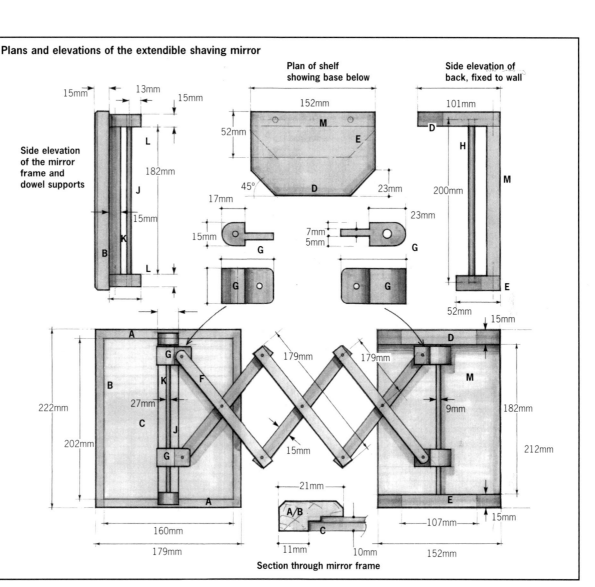

Plans and elevations of the extendible shaving mirror

Side elevation of the mirror frame and dowel supports

Plan of shelf showing base below

Side elevation of back, fixed to wall

Section through mirror frame

being offset. The lug at the
top at each end is offset one
way, and the one at the
bottom is offset
the other way by
the thickness of
the slat.

5 Drill the lugs
for the
dowel. One lug at
each end is a firm
fit and the other is
a loose fit so that
it can slide. Screw
the dowel
support (K), and

two dowel support brackets
(L) to the back of the mirror,
with the dowel held
between the brackets.
Likewise, drill the base (E)
and the shelf (D) for the rear
dowel. Now assemble the
back, shelf and base, with
the rear dowel and
extendible arm in position.
Repeat for the front, so that
the front dowel (J) is held
between the dowel brackets
(L), which are screwed to
the top and bottom of the
dowel support (K).

6 You should be able to
move the arm, with the
top two lugs sliding up and
down on the dowels. Fit a
piece of 3mm mirror into
the frame and screw the
mirror back (C) into the
frame as well.

7 It's wise to have done
some finishing before
you assemble the arm.
Remember it will get damp,
so varnish or oil are best.

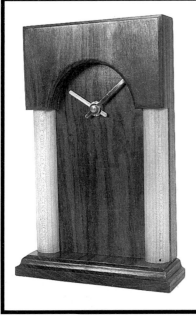

Find out how to make this solid timber clock with split columns that do not need a lathe.

HOW TO MAKE THE CLOCK

1 Plane up one plant of the wood you intend to use. The parts that make up the back, top and base are all the same thickness, though the base is that little bit wider.

2 Before you cut off the piece for the top, use a jigsaw, fretsaw, coping saw or bandsaw to make the arch. It is best if you can organise it so that the piece for the arch comes off the end of the piece for the back. That way the grain will match. Repeat for the base.

3 Cut off the arch piece and clean it up, ready to be glued to the back of the clock. Before you do that use a router and straight cutter (or chisel and mallet) to cut out the recess in the back for the quartz movement. Drill a hole for the spindle.

There are countless movements available, so make a recess to suit your type.

4 Line up the arch piece on the back so that the centre of the arch is on a line with the spindle hole. Use a square to check this, the

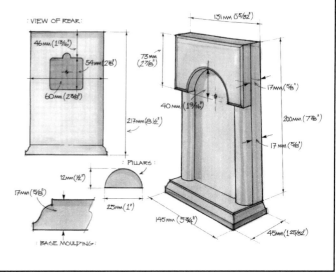

Details of the clock

arch held with a G-cramps. Do not glue yet. Mark the position for the arch and spread glue over it, using cramps to hold it.

5 The columns are a really neat trick. You might imagine that they need to be turned and split. Instead, use a router and radius cutter along the edge of a board. Once you have produced a radiused edge, you can cut a strip off the board which you can then

use as a column. In this case, maple was used for the columns as it contrasts well with the rosewood. Clean up the back of each column and glue them, overlong, to the back. Once the adhesive has set you can trim the upright columns.

CUTTING LIST

	LENGTH	WIDTH	THKNS
A Back(1)	200mm	131mm	17mm
B Arch(1)	73mm	131mm	17mm
A Base(1)	45mm	145mm	17mm
B Column(2)	127mm	25mm	12mm

Cut the arch on the end of your plank with a jigsaw. It helps to keep the board long at this stage, and by using the end the grain will hopefully match

Line up the arch with the spindle hole before gluing and assembling the back and arch. Pack the cramp to protect the wood

Rout or plane a radius along the edge of your board for the columns and then cut off a strip. The strips must be the same thickness to be the same width

HOW TO MAKE THE RACK

1 This design comprises of two pieces, one 1000x25x19mm and the other 600x80x19mm. Once prepared, cut the longer piece in half and the 600mm piece into five 90mm long pieces, one of which is used as the centre spine or spacer for the 'frame' of the rack.

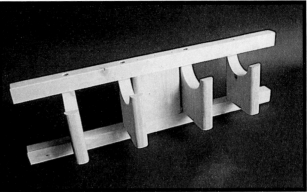

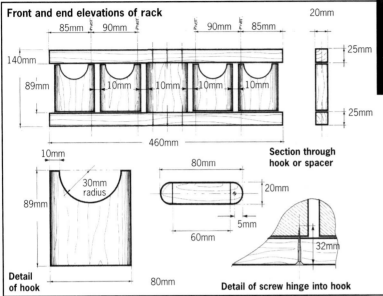

Front and end elevations of rack

85mm | 90mm | 90mm | 85mm | 20mm

140mm
89mm
25mm
25mm

10mm | 10mm | 10mm | 10mm

460mm

Section through hook or spacer

Detail of hook

10mm
30mm radius
89mm
80mm
80mm

80mm
20mm
5mm
60mm
32mm

Detail of screw hinge into hook

2 To profile the 'hook' on the pivoting hangers - either drill these with a tank cutter and cut afterwards, or cut first and bandsaw to the radius.

3 Prepare the two pieces to size first and then round over the hanger components with a router, and sand evenly.

4 Pin and glue the spacer first, which should be a little longer than the hooks to ensure that the hooks swing out. Then screw in the hooks.

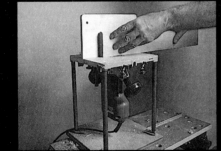

Mount a small router in a table with a rounding over cutter, to radius the edges on both sides of the hooks

Sand the ends of the hooks and spacer with a disc sander. The spaces must be a fraction longer

A 10mm wide bandsaw blade will be able to cut the radius you need on the towel rack hooks

Assemble the rails and spacer with glue and pins. It is worth leaving it in a G-cramp for the glue to set

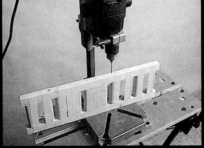

Wrap the assembly with masking tape for drilling hinge pilot holes, and then clearance holes in the rails

Countersink the holes then fix the screws before removing the tape and dismantling for finishing

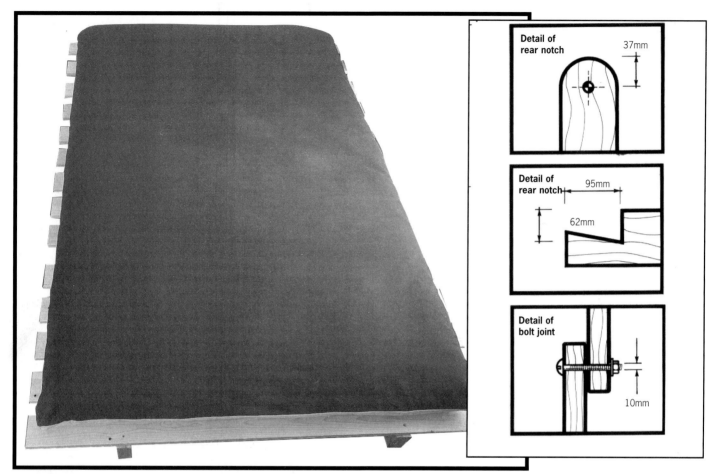

Detail of rear notch
37mm

Detail of rear notch
95mm
62mm

Detail of bolt joint
10mm

A combined bed and sofa.

HOW TO MAKE THE FUTON

1 Carefully select your timber, especially that which will make the seat bearers, as any twist or wind will cause problems when the futon is bolted up. Then cut two each of the seat bearers, back rests and back supports. If you buy long lengths of timber and cut carefully, you will be able to keep waste to a minimum.

2 Work out the bore holes carefully. Before you drill these, use the same centre for marking the radius on the back-rest and back support. Bore the holes to accept the 10mm (⅜in) roofing bolts. An 11mm (⁷⁄₁₆in) drill is best for this job. If you do not have one, use a 10mm (⅜in) drill and 8mm (⁵⁄₁₆in) bolts, which are still large enough. Use either a pillar drill or a brace and bit, but ensure that the holes are straight and true.

A mistake will mean that the components will not go together correctly.

3 Cut the six radii where necessary. Use a bandsaw, or a coping saw for this task. Bear in mind that the more care exercised here, the less cleaning up there will be later with glasspaper.

4 Cut the angle at the bottom of the back support and the notch at the rear of the seat pieces, which fit like a dovetail. When placed together after they have been cut, they should form a right angle. However, there is a bit of latitude here.

5 Before bolting the pieces together to form the side frames, take the arrises off. A bearing-guided rounding-over bit in a router will make short work of it and let you run around the radiused ends. If a router is not available then use a block plane or a spoke shave.

6 Sand all these components and bolt them together. Note that each end is handed: the back-rest sections need to go on the outside of the seat and back support bearers.

7 Put the prepared parts to one side while you work on the slats. Cut them all exactly 1,371mm (54in) long and again remove the arrises. Then drill and countersink for No. 10 screws.

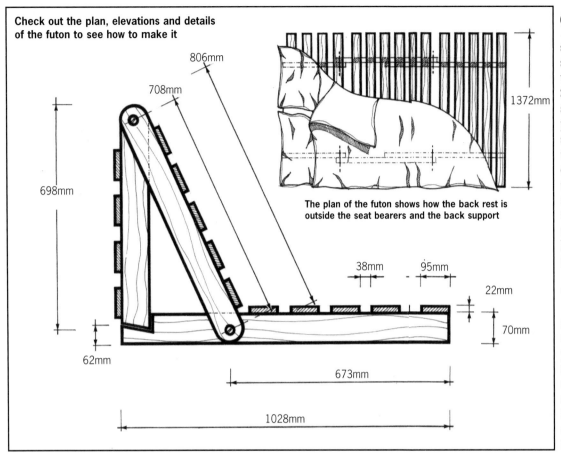

Check out the plan, elevations and details of the futon to see how to make it

806mm

708mm

698mm

62mm

673mm

1028mm

1372mm

The plan of the futon shows how the back rest is outside the seat bearers and the back support

38mm

95mm

22mm

70mm

9 Once the holes are drilled and the slat sanded, you can start to screw the whole thing together. Start by fixing the first slat onto the forward position of the seat section, ensuring that the overhang on each end is equal and that the slat is at right angles to the bearers. Continue like this until all the bearers have been fixed onto the seat.

10 Lay out the bed and fix on the rest of the slats, checking for square as you go. When all 14 slats have been attached, your futon is complete and ready to be varnished. To convert the sofa to a bed you simply lift the back support, laying the whole thing down, then unroll the mattress and place it over the base.

8 It is easiest to make a template flush with the end of the slat so that you know for certain that all the holes have been drilled in the right place. One word of warning though: five of the slats used for the centre section have their holes further outwards than the rest. This should be obvious from the assembled frames. Sand everything up, as it is an awkward task once the futon is assembled.

The end-grain will need sanding after it has been cut. The centre point for marking out the radius becomes the bolt hole

Removing the sharp arris on the edge of each component can be done with a router and rounding cutter, but a block plane will do

Cut out the notch on one end of the seat bearers, into which will fit the back support. This allows quick assembly

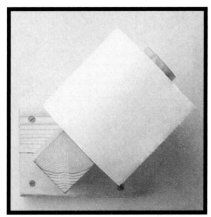

This simple idea is made from a short length of 50x50mm (2x2in) softwood, based on simple glue and screw methods, and using a saw, plane and drill. The arm of the holder can be positioned at any angle.

HOW TO MAKE THE TOILET ROLL HOLDER

1 Select and prepare to size a 406mm (16in) length of 'deal'. If it is roughsawn, carefully plane the sides and edges, checking squareness with a try square.

2 Mark out and cut to length the three main components; the base (A), the arm (B) and the holder (C).

3 Make the base piece by cutting component A in half (down the grain), marking first with a marking gauge and sawing with a tenon saw or using the bandsaw. Make the edges square (90°) and glue together to make a section of approximately 102x25mm (4x1in) - it will probably be just under. Use a PVA glue and clamp in the vice or with G-cramps. Clean up all surfaces of the base piece when glued and mark positions for the fixing holes, then drill and countersink.

4 Clean up all surfaces of the arm (component B), with a hand plane and disc sander if you have one. If the end grain is hand planed, a bevel can be planed all round to help prevent splitting.

5 To make the actual toilet roll holder, mark a circle (slightly smaller in diameter than the loo roll core) on both ends of the holder. Shade waste and then plane to a round section, holding firm in the vice. Use abrasive paper to get the final round section perfect.

6 Soften all edges on the three components by planing or sanding a bevel.

7 Drill, countersink, screw and glue the components together, taking care to wipe off excess glue. The arm can be positioned (by swivelling the screw) to the desired angle and then the glue allowed to set. The screws used are 65mm No. 10.

8 Apply two coats of polyurethane clear varnish, rubbing down in between coats.

9 With appropriate screws (brass or zinc plated to avoid rusting) fix the toilet roll holder to the wall, using rawl plugs.

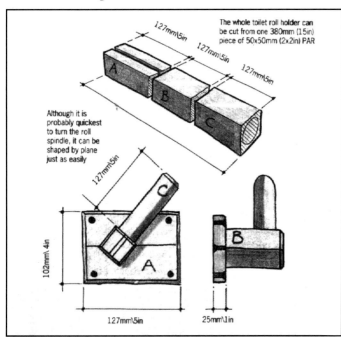

The whole toilet roll holder can be cut from one 380mm (15in) piece of 50x50mm (2x2in) PAR

127mm\5in
127mm\5in
127mm\5in

Although it is probably quickest to turn the roll spindle, it can be shaped by plane just as easily

127mm\5in

102mm\ 4in

127mm\5in

25mm\1in

The 50x50mm (2x2in) is cut in half down the grain, then joined along the edge to create the base piece

Circles are marked on each end and the round section easily achieved with a smoothing or jack plane

After cleaning up with a plane the base piece is drilled and countersunk for the support piece and wall screws

Fix the finished toilet roll holder to your bathroom wall with rust-resistant screws and rawl plugs

Make a rack for brushes and a beaker, secured to the wall by a housing joint batten.

CUTTING LIST			
	LENGTH	**WIDTH**	**THKNS**
A Batten(1)	171mm	36mm	21mm
B Holder(1)	171mm	100mm	21mm

HOW TO MAKE THE TOOTHBRUSH HOLDER

1 One good trick is to make the batten and the holder from the same piece of wood. If the joint between them is good, you'll hardly notice them as two pieces and people will wonder how you fixed it to the wall. Start by cutting the batten (A) off the back edge of the holder (B). Hold these two pieces together and mark a triangle across the join to identify the parts.

2 Plane the edges and set up a router to cut the dovetailed housing. You cut the housing first because that has to be determined by your cutter. You can then adjust the dovetailed tenon to fit. The best way to cut both parts of the joint is with a router, fitted under a table. This gives you so much more control than using the power-tool hand held. It is best to position the housing centrally, as that makes cutting the tenon so much easier later.

3 Having cut the housing, keep the dovetail cutter in the router, but adjust the fence. Make sure you have a few pieces the same thickness as the holder and batten, with which you can practise cutting the dovetailed tenon to fit the housing. You want to aim to cut each side of the holder to produce a symmetrical tenon. It is a case of adjusting the fence until it is spot on. When using the router table, make sure you have a guard to push the wood against the fence, to make your router table safer and more accurate.

4 Move now to drilling the holder for the brushes and the beaker. Once again, this is worth practising on scrap to guarantee all your brushes fit. The 15mm flat bit used seems to have done the trick for the brush holes. You can use a jigsaw or a hole saw for the beaker.

5 To clean up the piece, run a chamfer around the edges and around the holes. You may have to use a router cutter to do this. Then drill the batten for fixing screws and attach to the wall.

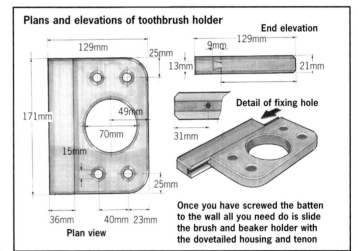

Plans and elevations of toothbrush holder

End elevation

129mm

9mm

13mm

21mm

129mm

25mm

171mm

49mm

70mm

15mm

31mm

Detail of fixing hole

25mm

36mm   40mm 23mm

Plan view

Once you have screwed the batten to the wall all you need do is slide the brush and beaker holder with the dovetailed housing and tenon

Cut the dovetailed housing in the batten first. Make sure that it is central on the edge.

When it comes to drilling the holes for the brushes, use a square as a guide if you have no pillar drill

Clean up with an abrasive flapwheel, then chamfer the edges and drill for the fixing screws

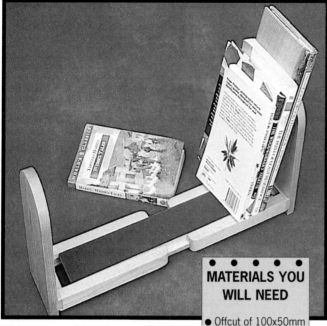

This unusual bookstand is made using hand-tools and a few offcuts.

MATERIALS YOU WILL NEED

● Offcut of 100x50mm softwood
● Baize for lining the central platform

HOW TO MAKE THE STAND

1 Mark out the components on timber (an offcut of 100x50mm(4x2in) softwood was used for this project) and cut out the end-plates. Plane the other parts to thickness, making sure that everything is square. A shooting board will help you to trim the ends of the end-plates. Cut the other components to length, then mark the positions of the cross-pieces.

2 Shape the end-plates, either by cutting a simple clipped diagonal from one of the corners, or by using a coping saw to curve the top. Sand smooth. Square off the middle platform block. You can use a combination plane to cut the rebates, but a router would be quicker.

3 Joint the ends of the platform to form the tongue, which fills the slot in the cross-rail of the end-plate when the stand is closed.

4 Cut the runners and rebate by hand, or with a router. Clean up, then cut the runners to length. Cross pieces are cut from left-over rebated runner material.

5 The runner components form a U-shape, with the thin fillet below the rebate.

The ends are jointed by halving, interlocking the rebates to increase the glued area. Fix the runner parts together, using the platform as a guide. Before gluing and clamping, lay a double thickness of paper between the runners and platform, for a loose sliding fit when set.

6 Turn the platform over. Mark out lengths of thin wooden fillets to glue over the bottom of the runners, to form the channel. Glue the thin strips across the bottom of the runners and add the longer side strips.

7 Ensure the underside is smooth and flat by rubbing it across a large sheet of abrasive paper. Chamfer the lower edge of the thin strip, underneath the runners, when they fit into the housings in the end-plates. Mark and chisel out the end-plate housings. Sand all surfaces smooth and apply a coat of sanding sealer / wax, avoiding the surfaces to be glued. Glue the end-plates to the runner assembly and check for squareness.

8 Check the fit of the runners on the platform, adjusting if necessary. It is better if they are loose rather than too

Plan, elevations and details to make a bookshelf

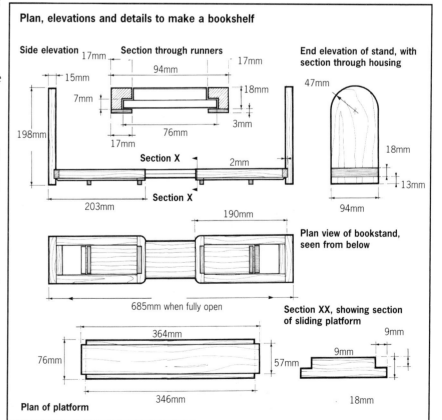

Side elevation
17mm
Section through runners
17mm
End elevation of stand, with section through housing
47mm
15mm
94mm
7mm
18mm
198mm
76mm
3mm
17mm
Section X
2mm
18mm
203mm
Section X
13mm
94mm
685mm when fully open
190mm
Plan view of bookstand, seen from below
Section XX, showing section of sliding platform
9mm
9mm
364mm
76mm
57mm
346mm
18mm
Plan of platform

tight. Even if the rebates are very loose, the feet will prevent any sagging. Fit the small foot across the inner end of each runner assembly and check that it stands squarely.

9 Now you need to cut a foot to fit between the side runners, under the platform. For the assembly to stand flat, this foot's depth has to be that of the small foot, plus the thickness of the fillets on the bottom of the rebates. To get this, turn the assembly upside-down and lay a straight edge along the bottom.

The distance from the bottom of the platform to the straight edge is the thickness you need for the little foot.

10 Position the foot at the platform's ends and glue in place. Repeat this operation for the other side. This foot also acts as a stop for the sliding platform, and therefore it is important to wax and finish the platform and runners first. Cut the baize for the underside of the feet and the end-plates, and also for the top of the platform if you so desire.

CUTTING LIST					
MATERIAL		**QTY**	**LENGTH**	**WIDTH**	**THKNS**
A End-plate	Softwood	2	300mm	93mm	15mm
B Middle platform	Softwood	1	356mm	76mm	17mm
C Runner	Softwood	4	180mm	18mm	18mm
D End runner	Softwood	2	93mm	18mm	18mm
E Side fillet	Softwood	4	170mm	16mm	3mm
F End fillet	Softwood	2	93mm	16mm	3mm
G Platform foot	Softwood	2	59mm	10mm	12mm
H Foot	Softwood	2	59mm	7mm	9mm

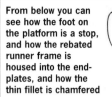

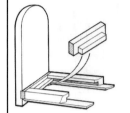

From below you can see how the foot on the platform is a stop, and how the rebated runner frame is housed into the end-plates, and how the thin fillet is chamfered

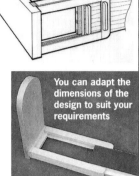

You can adapt the dimensions of the design to suit your requirements

Use a combination plane, or router, to rebate the platform, and for the runners, which can be cut off later

The same rebated runner strip is used for the end runners too.
Note that the rebates interlock

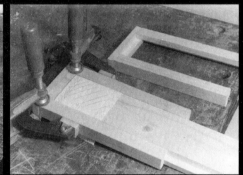

When gluing up the runner frames, use the platform to form them, wrapped in paper so it will still run

Glue fillets underneath the rebated runners to keep the platform in place and hold the runner ends firm

Mark out the housings on the end-plates, cut the shoulders and remove the waste with a chisel

Fix the feet to the platform with Superglue. There is no turning back now, so wax the sliding platform first

This spice rack is designed to take 14 small jars.

HOW TO MAKE THE SPICE RACK

The rack is made from a 2134mm (7ft) length of 75x18mm (3x¾in) PAR softwood. The dimensions are not hard and fast as the size of the rack will depend on which brand of spice you use and on the number of jars. Allow about 13mm (½in) clearance above the jars for getting them in and out of the rack.

1 Having decided on the dimensions, prepare the material to size. Use a try square to check that the ends are square. If they aren't, trim them with a block plane or a table disc sander.

2 Mark out the positions of the housing joints if you are using them, copying the marks from one piece to the other. If you choose the butt jointing method, drawing lines across the wood with a square and pencil will help locate the pieces at the gluing and pinning stage. Shade the waste wood.

3 Cut the housing joints on the upright pieces, using either a tenon saw and chisel or a router against a clamped batten. Alternatively, a radial arm saw will take them out in seconds.

4 Mark out the curves on the uprights and cut them with a coping saw, a jigsaw or a bandsaw, working very close to the line. Chisel or plan the corner radii at top and bottom.

5 Clean up the curves with abrasive paper wrapped round a suitable former. Try to keep the edges square.

6 Check that the lengths of the shelves are correct and identical, then assemble the uprights and three shelves. Apply a little glue, check the construction is square, and then pin it together. When the glue has dried, punch the pinheads in and apply a little filler to each of the holes.

7 Cut two 20mm (¹³/₁₆in) fillet strips by ripping down the middle of the remaining length of material and planing the sawn sides smooth. Drill and counter-sink a hole in each of the strips.

8 Glue the two fillet strips into place at the back of the spice rack. These act both as stops for the jars and as wall brackets. Only the tiniest G-cramps will fit in. If you don't have any, you can improvise by holding them in place, with offcut wedges in between each fillet and the shelf above. Clean up and varnish.

CUTTING LIST

	LENGTH
Softwood	2134x70x15mm

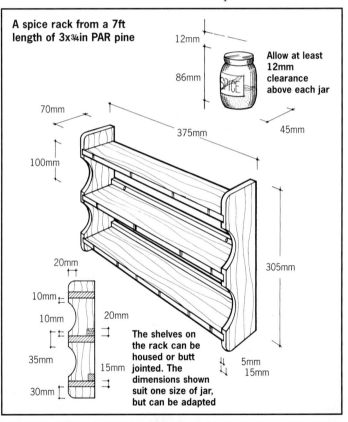

A spice rack from a 7ft length of 3x¾in PAR pine

12mm
86mm
Allow at least 12mm clearance above each jar

70mm
375mm
45mm
100mm
305mm
20mm
10mm
10mm
20mm
35mm
15mm
30mm
5mm
15mm

The shelves on the rack can be housed or butt jointed. The dimensions shown suit one size of jar, but can be adapted

When marking the joints on the uprights mark both together

Cut the joint shoulders with a tenon saw, and chisel out waste

Hold uprights together, and sand curves with abrasive on a former

With housing joints it is easy to assemble the shelves with pins

Making light pulls

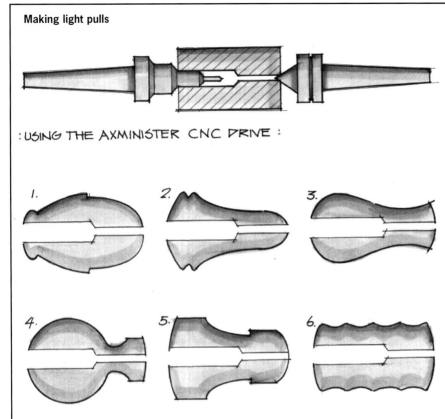

: USING THE AXMINISTER CNC DRIVE :

: SUGGESTED PROFILES :

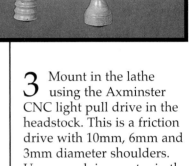

Here is a quick way to make attractive light pulls.

HOW TO MAKE THE LIGHT PULLS

1 Cut the blank, about 35mm diameter and 50mm long. Drill a 3mm hole for the cord, with a drillstand or in the lathe itself.

2 Drill the 6mm knot hole. You will have to experiment with the depth of this hole, so that the light pull hangs well but the cord is hidden from view.

3 Mount in the lathe using the Axminster CNC light pull drive in the headstock. This is a friction drive with 10mm, 6mm and 3mm diameter shoulders. Use a revolving centre in the tailstock, using that pressure to drive by friction.

4 Turn the light pull at about 2000rpm. Providing gentle cuts are made, with a sharp gouge, the friction drive will be sufficient. It may be necessary to increase tailstock pressure from time to time.

5 To finish, wax the light pull and attach the cord.

Shape the piece with a roughing gouge. As long as your cuts are not too deep and your gouge is sharp the CNC friction drive will not slip

Clean up the bottom of the light pull. The design of the drive enables you to turn right up to the edge of the hole. Some prefer oval skews for this kind of work

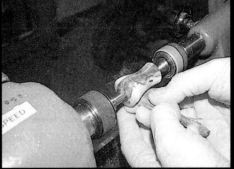

When it comes to sanding the piece note that the tool post must be moved right away, and that the abrasive must be held, of course, underneath the work

3 Cut the housing joints separately and make a guide with a piece of 18mm (¾in) thick MDF. This reduces the chance of the router jumping out.

4 Rout the housing joints 13mm (½in) wide and 6mm

(¼in) deep and then rout the back rebates 4mm (5/32in) wide and 6mm (¼in) deep to take the back panel. Rebate the front edge of the sides, below the bottom shelf, to take the ends of the front plinth.

For the rebating, a side fence can be fitted instead of using a straightedge guide.

5 Cut the sides to shape on a bandsaw, although a jigsaw or hardpoint panel saw could be used instead. Mark out the front plinth,

using a template for the curves and cut to shape. Cut the three shelves to length and width using a hardpoint saw.

6 Assemble the bookcase using PVA wood-working adhesive and 40mm long moulding pins, 1.8mm diameter. Drill pilot holes in the sides for the pins, from the inside to the outside, with a 1.5mm drill to make sure that they go in fair and square. The pins hold the wood together while the glue sets, but are

This simple bookcase is made from MDF with parana pine edging. Medium density fibreboard is particularly good for this project as it is strong, easy to work and fairly cheap.

HOW TO MAKE THE BOOKCASE

1 Mark out the side pieces for the shelf housings, the back rebates and slope.

2 The routing is done before shaping the bookcase sides. Cut the housing joints with a router, fitted with a TCT two-flute cutter.

You could make a guide from Formica-covered MDF, and cramp it to the wood 48mm (1⅞in) from the start of the housing joint. The MDF and guide are in turn cramped securely to the workbench.

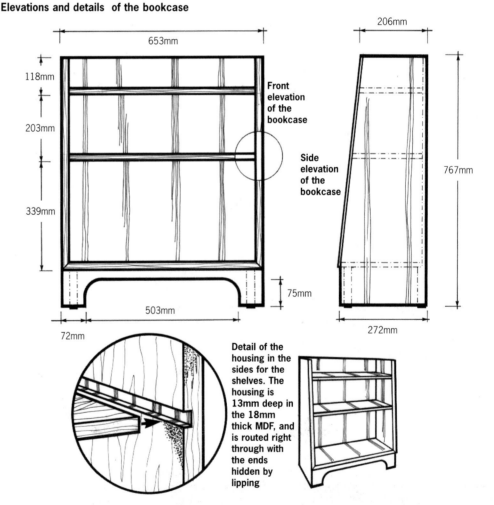

Elevations and details of the bookcase

653mm

118mm

203mm

339mm

72mm

503mm

Front elevation of the bookcase

Side elevation of the bookcase

206mm

767mm

272mm

75mm

Detail of the housing in the sides for the shelves. The housing is 13mm deep in the 18mm thick MDF, and is routed right through with the ends hidden by lipping unnecessary if you have sash cramps.

7 When the glue is dry, centre-punch each moulding pin down into the MDF and fill the hole with plastic wood filler. Sand the filler off with fine abrasive paper when it has hardened.

8 Make glue blocks from 25x25mm (1x1in) pine and glue them to the underside of the bottom shelf to support the front plinth.

Cut glue blocks 1mm (1/32in) longer than the carcase for the corner bracket feet so that the whole weight is taken on the blocks.

9 Cut the parana pine edging 7mm (9/32in) thick, with a circular saw, to match the widths of the front of the side panels and the front of the shelves. Use a fine-tooth combination blade to produce a smooth, almost planed finish on the pine. If you do not have a circular saw, you could consider buying a prepared strip from a DIY outlet. This could be moulded if you want. Glue and pin the edging into position and when the glue has set, centre punch and fill the holes.

10 Trim the back panel to fit exactly and glue a strip of pine edging along the top edge. Wait until you've painted it before you finally pin the panel into position, as this gives a better result than pinning first. Make sure you cover all the pine with masking tape before you paint the carcase.

11 Apply a coat of white acrylic primer and, when the bookcase is dry, rub it down well. Paint on two coats of gloss, rubbing down between coats. When the work is dry, remove the tape from the pine and apply two coats of satin varnish to the edging. Rub this down and wax-polish it with fine wirewool. Then pin the back panel in the rebates in the sides.

	MATERIAL	QTY	LENGTH	WIDTH	THKNS
A	Side MDF	2	760mm	270mm	18mm
B	Shelf MDF	3	630mm	270mm	12½mm
C	Front MDF plinth	1	630mm	120mm	6mm
D	Back MDF	1	760mm	630mm	3mm
E	Lipping Parana pine	1	760mm	250mm	25mm

CUTTING LIST

1 Mark out the two side pieces. If the supplier cut the MDF you will have little shaping to do, but do check for squareness

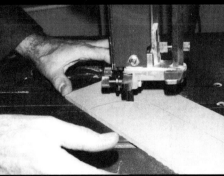
2 Rout the shelf rebates before cutting the sides. Routing two pieces together will save time, but beware of movement

3 Cutting each housing joint separately is less risky. An unfaced MDF guide is also less likely to slip than melamine-faced board

4 After routing a rebate for the back panel, cut the sides to shape with a bandsaw, jigsaw or a hardpoint panel saw

5 The curves on the front plinth match those on the child's storage chest. Use a bandsaw, jigsaw or coping saw

6 Lipping with parana pine is worth the extra work, instead of using MDF filler. Cut it on a circular saw or buy prepared strips

A lockable cabinet for the storage of medicines

CUTTING LIST

		LENGTH	WIDTH	THKNS
A	Top(1)	381mm	136mm	16mm
B	Bottom(1)	346mm	125mm	16mm
C	Side(2)	432mm	125mm	16mm
D	Shelf(1)	340mm	107mm	12mm
E	Frieze(1)	360mm	42mm	16mm
F	Door(1, ply)	319mm	327mm	12mm
G	Back(1)	337mm	346mm	6mm

One pair of 32mm hinges
One 32mm lock

HOW TO MAKE THE CABINET

1 As the cabinet may well be painted you can use almost anything to make it. Medium density fibreboard (DF) or prepared softwood (PAR) are the most suitable. Prepare the sides (C), top (A), bottom (B) and shelf (D) first. Mark out the housing joints in the sides for the bottom and the shelf. Also mark for the rebate along the top edge of the sides and the housing in the top for the sides.

2 Cut the housings in the sides, 8mm deep, and the rebate on the top edge to produce a tongue on the inner edge 8mm long and 8mm deep. If painting the cabinet, the rebate can run the full width of the side.

3 Cut the top (A) 10mm overlength so that you have enough for rounding over later. Chisel or rout out the 8mm wide, 8mm deep rebate for the sides. This must stop short of the front

edge, so you can round over the top. Also, cut out a recess from the top to hide the key.

4 Dry assemble the carcase, cutting the bottom and shelf the same length as the distance from outer edge to outer edge of the housings, for the sides under the top. Take apart and cut a rebate from the back edges of the sides, top and bottom to take the back (G). The rebate needs to be 6mm deep and 8mm wide.

5 Shape the bottom of the sides with a coping saw or fretsaw. Round the front and side edges of the top with a block

plane or a rounding over bit in a router. For a small job like this, you will probably find the plane just as quick. Assemble the carcase with glue, pinning the joints with 32mm panel pins. Check for square by measuring the diagonals. Once set, knock the pin heads down with a punch, and fill.

6 Attach the frieze before fixing the back, by screwing up through the top. Pin the back into the rebate and to the shelf with 25mm pins.

7 Cut out the solid ply or MDF door (you could make a framed door), allowing a 1.5mm gap all round for three coats of paint. Fit a lock, and cut a keep (recess) in the side for the lock latch. Paint the piece, fit an escutcheon and fix to the wall with 32mm screws.

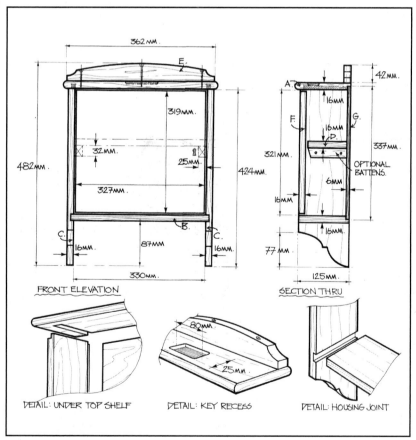

FRONT ELEVATION

SECTION THRU

DETAIL: UNDER TOP SHELF

DETAIL: KEY RECESS

DETAIL: HOUSING JOINT

HOW TO MAKE A RACK FOR FRUIT AND VEGETABLES

1 Start by planing up the stock for the sides. The sides have been decorated with a curve to top and bottom edges, to reflect the curves of the dowel racks. The curved cut-out at the bottom produces a pair of feet.

2 Mark out and drill the holes for the dowel. Find the centre line on the sides first and then use a pair of compasses to mark out the racks.

3 Cut the dowel to length - for this project, 10mm dowel was used. Set up a stop on your bench hook, mitre saw or tablesaw for consistent length.

4 Assemble the vegetable rack - the dowels go through the sides and you will need to cut some pieces of scrap to match the width

1 Cut the top of the sides to a curve. Note the shoulder at the end of the curve, to mirror the feet at the base

2 Drill the holes for the dowel racks with a flat bit. Hold the sides together with a cramp to drill both at the same time

3 To produce wedges to hold the dowel firmly, make a series of cuts with the grain, then cut them off across the grain

of the rack. Make lots of little wedges, cut a slot in each end of each rod. Smear the ends with glue, assemble using cramps and the spacers and knock in the wedges. Once dry, plane the dowel ends flush. It is best to finish the sides and the rods before assembly. Ramin dowel smells horrible and fruit can get damp, so varnish all the parts before using the rack.

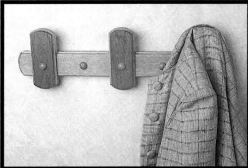

HOW TO MAKE THE COAT RACK

1 Start by making the hooks. For contrast, you could stick a thin layer of walnut to a thicker piece of oak. It is actually easier to stick together two pieces of equal thickness, as a long strip from which you can cut three hooks. Once the glue has gone off, plane up the edges square and cut off the excess walnut with a bandsaw, before planing it to thickness.

2 Cut the three hooks to length, and use a pair of compasses to make the radius top and bottom. Cut the curves on a bandsaw or with a jigsaw or coping saw. Make sure the curves are smooth.

3 To make full use of the contrasting wood, you need to mould the edge of the hooks. Form a simple radius, using a bearing-guided radius cutter. You could use a moulding plane, or a router table.

4 Plane up the stock for the rack batten. The rear face is angled to 15° to bring the hooks away from the wall. Plane the piece square first and then cut away and plane the angle. Use a marking gauge to batten to make a line around the batten to which you can plane.

5 Rout the moulding around the front face of the batten with the same cutter you have used for the hooks. It is best to do this before you cut the housing for the hooks, otherwise the cutter can wander and potentially mar the wood.

6 Take one of the hooks as a guide for the housings on the batten. Use a marking gauge to draw a depth line for cutting the shoulders.

7 Use a chisel to pare away the waste from the housing and test the fit. Drill through the housing and screw the hooks home.

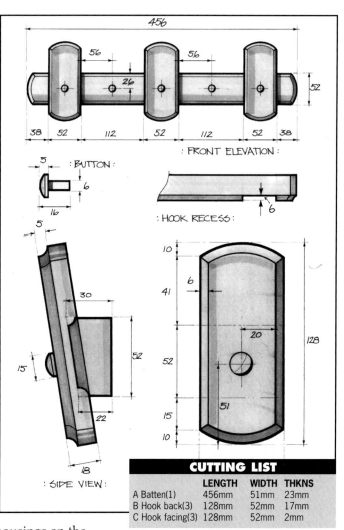

: FRONT ELEVATION :

: BUTTON :

: HOOK RECESS :

: SIDE VIEW :

CUTTING LIST			
	LENGTH	WIDTH	THKNS
A Batten(1)	456mm	51mm	23mm
B Hook back(3)	128mm	52mm	17mm
C Hook facing(3)	128mm	52mm	2mm

Cut the three hooks to length and mark on the back, with compasses, the radiused curve

Mark out the bevel on the back of the batten, cut off most of the excess, then plane it smooth

Use the finished hooks to mark the shoulders of the housings.
Then pare away the waste with a chisel

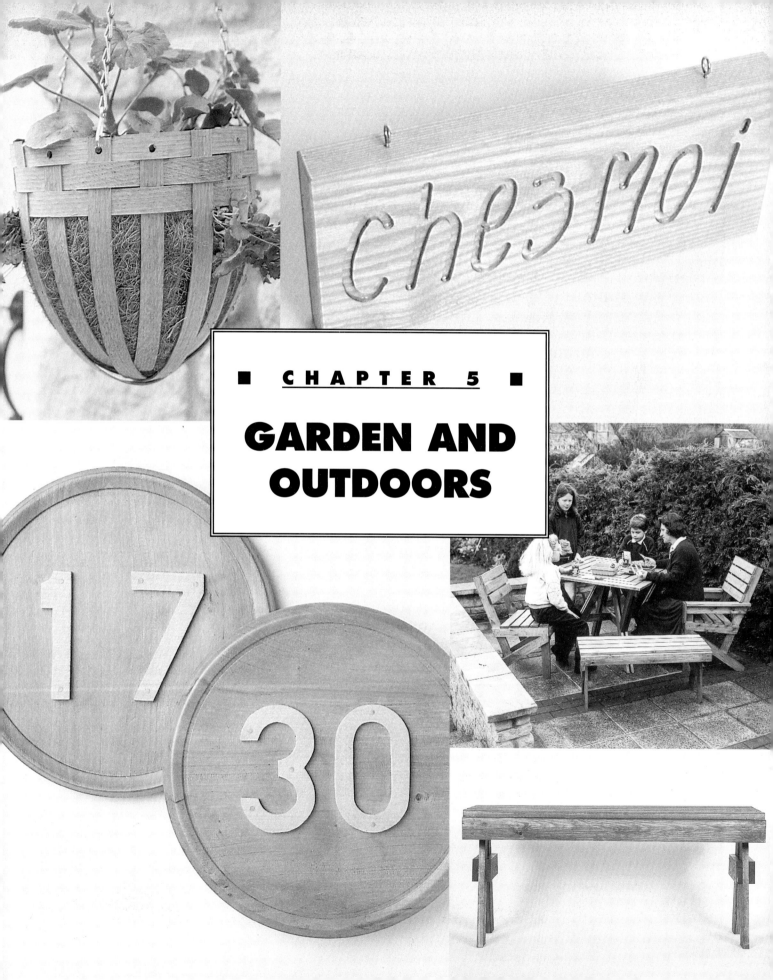

CHAPTER 5

GARDEN AND OUTDOORS

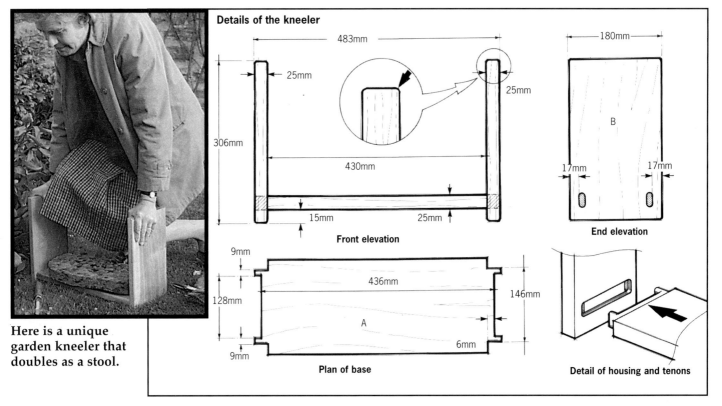

Details of the kneeler

483mm

25mm

306mm

430mm

25mm

15mm

25mm

Front elevation

180mm

B

17mm

17mm

End elevation

9mm

436mm

128mm

146mm

A

9mm

6mm

Plan of base

Detail of housing and tenons

Here is a unique garden kneeler that doubles as a stool.

HOW TO MAKE THE GARDEN KNEELER

1 Plane up one plank of the wood you intend to use. The parts that make up the base (A) and the sides (B) are all the same thickness. The sides are a bit wider than the base.

2 Cut the base to width. This is as easily done by hand as it is by jigsaw, bandsaw or tablesaw. If you do not own any power-tools or a machine, sawing wood along the grain (ripping) is likely to be the operation that persuades you to buy a jigsaw or bandsaw.

3 Chisel or rout out the stopped housing in the side. Then cut the pair of mortices. Use a router for this, hence the mortices have rounded corners, but it won't take much longer to work by hand.

4 Cut the notches at each side of the base so that

it will fit into the stopped housing. The housing does not have to be very deep, but the full thickness of the base.

5 Offer up the base to each side to mark out the tenons. Cut the tenons and dry assemble then glue up the kneeler.

Having cut the housing and the mortices round over the edges with a router and guided cutter

When cutting the tenons the outer cut is longer than the inner cut to take account for the end notches

If you have routed out the mortices you will need to file the tenons round to fit. Check regularly

Use a species of wood that has straight grain. That way when you cut it into veneer and bend it the fibres are less likely to break. You can alter its size and shape easily to meet your needs.

HOW TO MAKE THE HANGING BASKET

1 Start by cutting the veneers. Alternatively you may choose to buy some. Oak bends pretty well. The safest way to cut veneers is with a bandsaw. Plane the edge of the board before each cut.

2 First you have to plane up your board to thickness. Then set the rip fence on your bandsaw to cut a strip about 2mm thick. The blade on your bandsaw has to be set perfectly square with the table. If not the strips will be all over the place. After cutting each strip, plane the leading edge of the board.

3 Cut a disc out of the centre of a piece of MDF or ply or chipboard. The disc and the circle are the nearest you'll get to a former.

4 For the weaving, replace the disc inside the MDF circle and start bending strips of veneer from one side to the other, having steamed them over a kettle. Once all the vertical strips are in position, start weaving the horizontal parts.

A novel way to weave a hanging basket for small plants by cutting narrow oak veneers

Use a kettle to soften the fibres for bending. You have no former, so they need to be pliable

Cut a disc out of a piece of MDF. The bent strips of veneer fit in the sawcut in the MDF

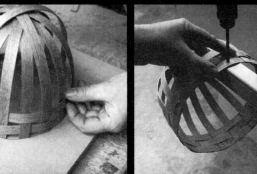

Continue the weaving, alternating the weave. When you finish one layer you hide it behind a vertical

Drill the basket for the chains by resting it on a piece of scrap. You need three holes

Start with the top layer (that is nearest the open end). Hide the join under one of the verticals and hold with a spot of glue. Then drill three holes for the chains which are attached with a simple spring clasp.

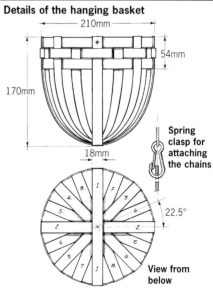

Details of the hanging basket

210mm

54mm

170mm

18mm

Spring clasp for attaching the chains

22.5°

View from below

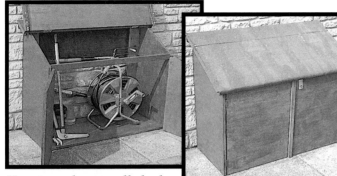

How to make a small shed for forks, spades and more.

HOW TO MAKE THE CUPBOARD

1 Start by cutting up the ply. This always needs careful planning. One trick is to use scale templates of the sheet and the parts to find the best arrangement for cutting. Consider altering the size and shape of the parts to suit the dimensions of a sheet of ply. The cupboard's length was determined by a standard garden fork. You only need to reduce the height a bit to get all the pieces from an 8x4ft sheet. All you need to do is have less of a pitch on the roof.

2 Once you have cut out the parts the construction is pretty simple,

with all the parts screwed and glued together using butt joints. Start by fixing the sides (A) to the base (B), and the top spacer (C) to the sides. Then screw the front rail (D) between the sides, using L brackets. Drill the dowel supports (E) and screw them to the sides, base and top spacer. Hinge the flap (F) to the top spacer and the doors (G) to the sides. Now screw the lipping to the flap and the ends of the top spacer. Screw a piece of lipping to one of the doors as a stop. You could finish the unit with a Sadolin preservative, with green roofing felt on the top and a clasp for security.

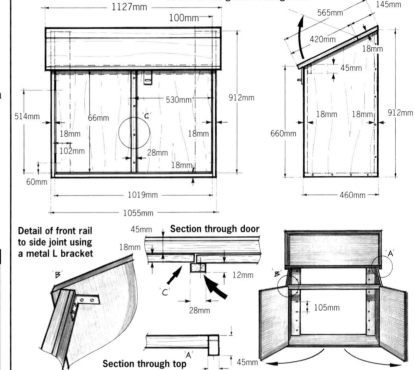

Details of the garden storage unit

Detail of front rail to side joint using a metal L bracket

Section through door

Section through top

CUTTING LIST

	LENGTH	WIDTH	THKNS
A Side (2)	912mm	460mm	18mm
B Base (1)	1019mm	460mm	18mm
C Top spacer (1)	1019mm	145mm	18mm
D Front rail (1)	1019mm	45mm	23mm
E Dowel support (2)	912mm	100mm	18mm
F Flap (1)	1081mm	420mm	18mm
G Door (2)	660mm	530mm	18mm
H Lipping (1)	2200mm	45mm	23mm
I Door lipping (1)	660mm	28mm	12mm

Start by screwing the sides to the base. Extend the base to the front edge of the sides so the doors are inside the base

Hinge the flap to the top spacer. Notice how the top spacer and the flap both overhang the sides and front of the unit

Screw lipping to the flap and the top. After fixing cut the lipping at the hinge line with a tenon saw

This project shows how to turn a house number plaque from a pearwood blank and cut the numbers from this sycamore to give a clear contrast.

HOW TO MAKE THE PLAQUE

1 Mark a 210mm (9¼ in) circle in the base hardwood and cut it roughly to the round using a bandsaw.

2 Make a glue chuck from a piece of 20mm (¾ in) thicknessed oak: cut it roughly in a circle of 110mm (4⅜ in). Screw the oak to a 100mm (4in) diameter faceplate with four No 12 20mm (¾ in) csk woodscrews. With the faceplate on the lathe, turn the outside of the glue chuck to round and check the face to see if it is running true.

3 Glue the pear blank to the glue chuck with 3 blobs of 100-second hot-melt adhesive. Cramp overnight for an effective bond. Screw the thicknessed blank straight onto the faceplate, but make sure you do not cut through to the screw ends when you are turning.

4 Make sure your lathe is set on a slow speed, then turn an 8mm (5⁄16 in) rim using a 9mm (⅜ in) spindle gouge. Turn the recessed front with the same gouge followed by a gentle cut with a 25mm (1in) square-ended scraper. Switch off the lathe and check for flatness.

5 Sand the disc in the lathe, starting with 250 grit, then 400 grit, and finish with a final burnish using a handful of shavings. If the glue chuck methods are used the plaque can be eased off from the chuck with a wedged knife. Tap it gently with a hammer if necessary but remove it from the lathe to save the bearings. Peel off the hot-melt glue.

6 Drill a shallow 25mm (¼ in) hole for the keyhole plate in the back of the plaque at the top and fix it in place with brass screws.

7 For the numbers. trace round a 75mm (3in) Helix plastic number stencil onto a slice of 5mm (5⁄16 in) thick kiln-dried sycamore, which made a good contrast to the pear.

8 Cut out the number(s) using a powered fretsaw or coping saw.

Support the work with your fingers each side of the blade to stop the work jumping up.

9 Glue the numbers to the plaque with Cascamite or other waterproof adhesive, then put a weight on top of it and leave overnight. Dowelling in each number adds extra security.

Cut the blank for the plate on a bandsaw so that it is pretty close to the size you need

Mark on the blank's back a circle the size of your false faceplate, so that you know where to position it

Glue the blank to a wooden face on your faceplate, with either hot-melt or a glue paper joint

Turn the blank to round. If you do not have a lathe, use a coping saw and sand it afterwards

A broken fork is no more than an opportunity to do a little turning. To remove the shaft from the fork cut it off flush with the metal sleeve and then drill it out.

HOW TO TURN THE HANDLE

1 First measure inside the tool handle for the spigot with a Vernier gauge. Turn down the spigot with a 12mm (½ in) skew chisel.

2 Starting from the top end of the handle, turn a bead over left and right, then produce a flat section to the bead with the skew. This will eventually be the hollow.

3 Turn another bead beyond the flat section, with another flat for a hollow.

4 Shape the top 50mm (2in) of the handle part of the shaft down to the beads and flats.

5 Turn the coves with a fingernail gouge, downhill from either side to the bottom of each cove, starting with the gouge on its side and twisting it as you go.

6 With the gouge still to hand, turn down the tapered section to a fraction over the finished size, through you may prefer to use a skew for a fine finish straight off the chisel.

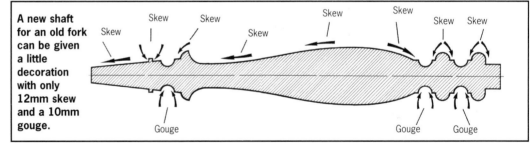

A new shaft for an old fork can be given a little decoration with only 12mm skew and a 10mm gouge.

Skew Skew Skew Skew Skew Skew Skew Skew

Gouge Gouge Gouge

Mark all the divisions on the fork shaft having roughed it to a cylinder

Use a fingernail gouge to shape the coves, working down from the high points

Finish the gentle sweep of the handle with a skew chisel, using only the lower portion

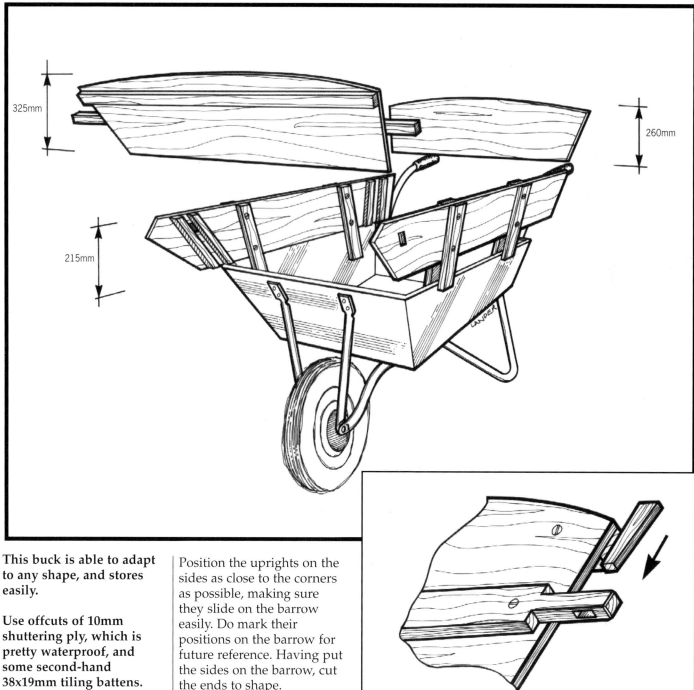

325mm

260mm

215mm

This buck is able to adapt to any shape, and stores easily.

Use offcuts of 10mm shuttering ply, which is pretty waterproof, and some second-hand 38x19mm tiling battens.

HOW TO MAKE A BARROW BUCK

1 Cut the sides to shape first and then screw and glue on the battens.

Position the uprights on the sides as close to the corners as possible, making sure they slide on the barrow easily. Do mark their positions on the barrow for future reference. Having put the sides on the barrow, cut the ends to shape.

2 Do not worry too much about the tricky compound angles. The end nearest the gardener slots between two battens screwed to each side.

3 The front piece has a batten screwed across it, extending about 75mm (3in) at each side to push through a mortice in the

sides. It can then be wedged in place to keep the buck together, with the wedges on a retaining cord.

HOW TO MAKE A SIGN

1 Select a piece of hardwood and plane the side flat, supporting it against a benchstop if it is too wide to fit in a vice. This type of timber is more difficult to bruise and damage.

2 Put the wood in the vice and plane the edge flat and square.

By this stage you need to have planned your sign and will know what size of board you need. The sign's length will depend on the number of letters. Divide the length into equal measurements with spaces between words, then draw the name freehand.

3 Plane the ends. Fix the wood to the bench for routing, either between dogs or with hot-melt glue. Fit a router with a straight cutter of 6mm (¼ in) diameter or less, and set the depth to about two-thirds its diameter. Large cutters are harder to control when you are routing freehand.

4 The action is to plunge the cutter to full depth at one end of each letter and carefully control the router, following the drawn letter shape and guiding the router with both hands. At the end of the letter shape, withdraw the cutter without moving the router as you let off the plunge-lock mechanism. While holding the base, lift one hand to unlock the plunge, while the other keeps the router steady.

5 Clean up the block with a hand plane an abrasive paper, bevelling the edges slightly. Drill two small holes to take the eye hooks and brush on a weather-resistant lacquer or oil.

Plane against a wide stop, held on the workbench with a cramp, to support the piece across its width

Divide your board into equal parts, according to the number of letters and words on the nameplate

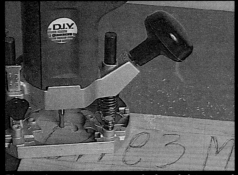

Plunge the router at one end of each letter and then follow the outline around the shape freehand

The end of each letter is the tricky part. Unlock the plunge with one hand and let up the router carefully

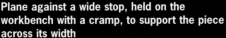

Make this simple trellis to disguise unsightly rainwater pipes.

HOW TO MAKE THE TRELLIS

1 You can use 12mm or 15mm square section timber for the trellis. It helps if all the parts are made from the same, but many of the dimensions will depend on the size and position of the pipe you want to cover. Select timber at least 2m long for each of the vertical parts (A) or to suit the length of pipe you are intending to cover.

2 Start by cutting the four uprights (A) to length. Mark out where you want to position the cross-pieces (B). These are all 150mm long, and the same square section as the uprights.

You could fit the frame together with halving joints, which takes more work, but perhaps more secure than pinned and glued butt joints.

3 You might also find it easier to screw the trellis together instead of nailing. Again this means more work, drilling countersunk clearance holes, and then pilot holes. The best way to do it is to pin and glue the side frames first. Leave these to set before joining them at the front with more cross-pieces.

You may find it easiest to use screws instead of nails. Tapping in nails can be disruptive, breaking the

joints you have already fixed. You will find it helps to have a spacer, like a tin, at this stage in the construction.

4 Naturally you cannot fit a four-side frame around a pipe fixed to a wall. The solution is to use loose cross-pieces at the back. These fit inside the

back uprights and over the side cross-pieces. Cut a notch from each end of the back cross-piece to fit over the side cross-pieces. This locks the trellis in place around the pipe.

5 Finish the trellis with light green undercoat, or you may prefer to use an exterior brand of treatment for timber.

CUTTING LIST			
	LENGTH	WIDTH	THKNS
A Upright (4)	2000mm	15mm	15mm
B Rail (20)	150mm	15mm	15mm

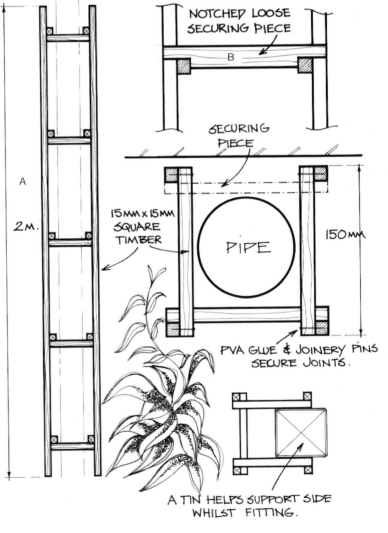

A
2M.

NOTCHED LOOSE SECURING PIECE
B

SECURING PIECE

15MM x 15MM SQUARE TIMBER

PIPE

150MM

PVA GLUE & JOINERY PINS SECURE JOINTS.

A TIN HELPS SUPPORT SIDE WHILST FITTING.

An attractive piece of garden furniture, quick and easy to make, based around a simple sandwich joint.

Elevation of frame measurements:
1340MM (52¾")
660MM (26")
20MM (25/32")
60MM (2³⁄₈")
70MM (2¾")
600MM (23⁵⁄₈")
'HALVING' JOINTS
790MM (31⅛")
740MM (29⅛")
35MM (1³⁄₈")
70MM (2¾")
70MM (2¾")
910MM (35¹³⁄₁₆")
310MM (12⁷⁄₃₂")
1055MM (41½")
965MM (38")
15MM (19/32")
70MM (2¾")

HOW TO MAKE THE TABLE

If you draw it all out it will be easier, but it is possible to assemble the leg frames by measuring the marking components positions.

1 Begin with the two cross frames, top and middle. Cross-half lengths of timber (A) and dry fit them.

2 Fit the two pairs of main diagonal legs (B) to catch part of the top cross-frame, making them meet up at the cross-halving joint.

3 The four pairs of arms (C) can be cut and their position marked. The lower ends of the arms sandwich the ends of the middle cross-frame parts (D).

4 Only one of the middle cross-frames must be fitted, glued and nailed to the arms and legs. If you fit

The top joint is a little complex, so lay it out on the floor. The top rails have a cross-halving joint, as will the lower rails

Try to get the butt joints between the braces and the legs as tight as possible. This helps to strengthen the table

You can assemble the underframe in two halves, except that you have to leave one of the lower rails till last

When you attach the top slats you will need to drill the nail holes first as they are close to the edge and could split

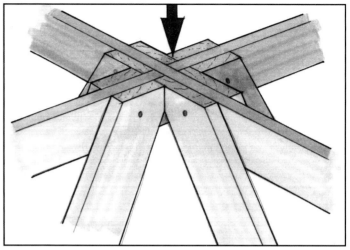

MATERIALS AND TOOLS YOU WILL NEED

- PAR - 30m (75mm wide and 25mm thick)
- Timber preservative
- Round wire nails (50mm)
- Glue

TOOLS
- Tape measure
- Square
- Saw
- Hammer
- Drill
- Plane
- Radial arm saw
- Handsaw

passer-by and the already completed frame standing vertically between you. Any other way you can devise of soundly hammering the second cross-rail into the now assembled leg frame will do.

6 Cut the top slats for the outside and inside. Glue and nail these on first, then arrange the spacing of the ones in between.Cut and fit these similarly. It is vital that you pre-drill the ends of these slats or the nails split the wood. Angle the hole slightly inwards so there is no risk of the nails emerging from the sides of the cross-frames. Pre-drill and nail the sides of the corners.

the middle rails to both frames, you will not be able to cross-half the frames together!

5 To fit the second middle rail, cross-halving into the first one, rest one end in position on the bench. The other end is supported by a

7 If the table wobbles, turn it upside-down and measure the distance from the top to the feet. Mark out on all of them the shortest of the four distances, hold a straight edge between

each pair of feet, line off and saw away. Now apply your finish.

8 The following two projects can be made to complete the garden set.

HOW TO MAKE A CHAIR

1 Draw out the side frames and cut components to length with a handsaw.

2 Mark, glue and nail the seat rails (A) to the front leg (B) of the chair.

3 Fit the diagonal back leg (C) into this joint, mark, glue and nail.

4 Mark, glue and nail the back (D) between the seat rails and back leg.

5 Nail the slats (E) on the seat, taking care over the spacing.

Each slat is glued to add sideways rigidity.

6 Chamfer the top front edges of the seat slats as with the bench overleaf.

MATERIALS YOU WILL NEED

- 12m of PAR (75mm wide and 25mm thick)
- Timber preservative
- Round wire nails (50mm)
- Glue

Cut out all the leg components. The front legs are made from one length, the diagonal back legs are each two

Always mark on the position of a joint before applying adhesive. For the chair side frame it will help to draw it in

Once the seat rail is pinned to the front leg and to the back upright, position it between the two back leg components

With the two side frames glued up and set you can join them together with the back and seat slats, again glued and pinned

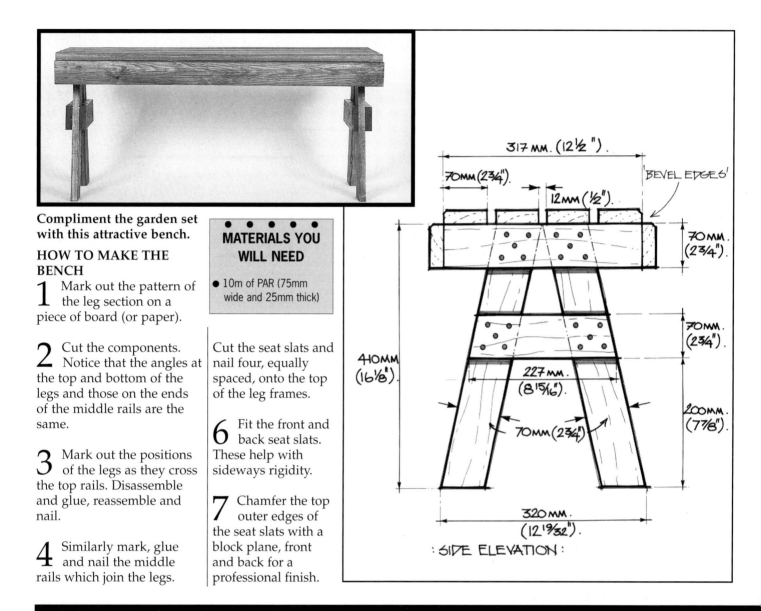

Compliment the garden set with this attractive bench.

HOW TO MAKE THE BENCH

1 Mark out the pattern of the leg section on a piece of board (or paper).

2 Cut the components. Notice that the angles at the top and bottom of the legs and those on the ends of the middle rails are the same.

3 Mark out the positions of the legs as they cross the top rails. Disassemble and glue, reassemble and nail.

4 Similarly mark, glue and nail the middle rails which join the legs.

MATERIALS YOU WILL NEED

● 10m of PAR (75mm wide and 25mm thick)

Cut the seat slats and nail four, equally spaced, onto the top of the leg frames.

6 Fit the front and back seat slats. These help with sideways rigidity.

7 Chamfer the top outer edges of the seat slats with a block plane, front and back for a professional finish.

: SIDE ELEVATION :

317 MM. (12½")
70MM (2¾").
12MM (½").
'BEVEL EDGES'
70 MM. (2¾").
410MM (16⅛")
70MM. (2¾").
227 MM. (8¹⁵/₁₆").
70MM (2¾")
200MM (7⅞").
320 MM. (12¹⁹/₃₂").

With the legs glued and nailed to one rail, offer up the second rail and mark its position so that you can return it accurately

To position the lower rail use a piece of scrap between the rails. Go through the same procedure of gluing and nailing

Having assembled the two end frames join them with the four seat slats. Tap the tip of each nail first to stop it splitting the wood

HOW TO MAKE THE FLYING DUCK

1 Start by cutting out the duck body shape (A). If you use ply paint it to protect it from the elements. Drill this for the 20mm diameter piece of dowel (D) to join the wings.

2 Cut out the four wings (B). Each pair of wings fits onto a coupling block (C). Each wing fits in a slot cut in the end of the block. The wings are at 90° to each other to produce a propeller. Cut the slots in the blocks. Then drill the blocks to accept a brass bush. This brass bush (E) allows the wing to revolve easily on a screw. The screw fits through the brass bush and screws into the piece of dowel (D) that is fitted through the hole in the duck body, with a washer on either side of the block. Drill the bottom of the duck with a 30mm bit for the rod.

3 Paint the body and the wings and assemble the whole duck. To make the spinning assembly for the top of the mounting rod (F), drill the end of the mounting rod to take a 3mm diameter piece of welding rod. Drop a washer or bush over this and then a piece of 5mm diameter brass tube (H), which fits into the bottom of the duck body. Stick the brass tube into the duck body with glue. Stick in the ground.

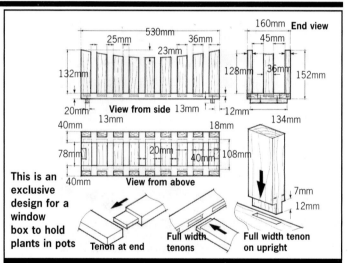

This simple idea, made mostly from plywood adds a bit of fun to windy days.

CUTTING LIST

	LENGTH	WIDTH	THKNS
A Body (1)	400mm	137mm	13mm
B Wing (4)	195mm	97mm	13mm
C Coupling block (2)	110mm	25mm	25mm
D Central dowel (1)	140mm	20mm	20mm
E Brass bush (2)	25mm	5mm	5mm
F Mounting rod (1)	500mm	20mm	20mm
G Welding rod (1)	80mm	3mm	3mm
H Brass tube (1)	50mm	5mm	5mm

HOW TO MAKE THE WINDOW BOX

1 This is an exercise in cutting mortices and tenons where you set up machines and produce the joints on a repetitive basis. Use a router table for the tenons and a hollow mortice chisel to make the holes. The lower frame of slats (C) and rails (B) is all of the same thickness and width. The uprights (A) are slightly narrower.

2 Start by cutting the mortices. Leave the rails overlong at this stage, and note that all the tenons are full width, bar the end ones. These have a short shoulder on the outside edge so that you do not see the tenon in the end of the rails. All the other tenons are full width.

3 Having cut the mortices for the slats and the uprights, mark out the tenons. Do a sample tenon first. From the sample tenon you can start setting up your machinery.
Use a router table, with a straight cutter in the router. Slide the workpiece over the cutter, with the wood held in a jig, and against the fence.

4 Assemble the box without glue to make sure it all fits. Glue up the bottom frame of slats and rails. Then glue in the uprights. When dry, cut the uprights to length. Finally screw a pair of feet under the slats and oil the box.

CUTTING LIST

	LENGTH	WIDTH	THKNS
A Upright (20)	132mm	36mm	17mm
B Rail (2)	530mm	40mm	20mm
C Slat (9)	108mm	40mm	17mm

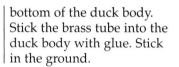

This is an exclusive design for a window box to hold plants in pots

Tenon at end

Full width tenons

Full width tenon on upright

Glue up the rails and slats, now add the uprights.. The tenons are the same length as on the slats

Cramp a backing strip of softwood to the uprights and then trim them with a jigsaw. The backing strip protects the uprights as you cut

An easy way to make a tray for milk bottles, which will look good on any doorstep.

HOW TO MAKE THE BOTTLE TRAY

1 Start with the sides, which are dovetails, and drilled for the dowel and divider.

2 Cut the dovetails on the sides of the tray. Dry assemble the sides and mark the position of the divider. Cut the mortices for the divider tenons in the sides of the tray.

3 Drill two of the sides and the dowel rails. Note that the holes in the sides stop halfway so that they cannot be seen.

4 Assemble the tray with the dowels in place. Then drill the handle

supports for the dowel handle. Attach the supports to the tray with brass screws

in little cups. Finish with a weather-resistant lacquer or oil.

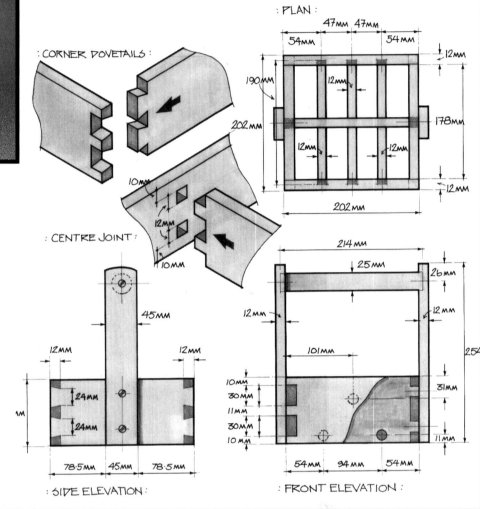

: CORNER DOVETAILS :

: CENTRE JOINT :

: PLAN :

: SIDE ELEVATION :

: FRONT ELEVATION :

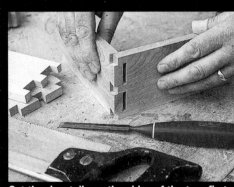

Cut the dovetails on the sides of the tray first. You need nothing more than a tenon saw and a small chisel

Drilled stopped holes in two of the sides for the dowel rails. There are two rails on which the bottles sit

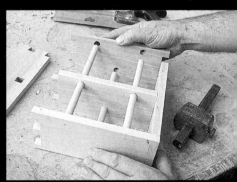

Assemble the tray, not forgetting the dowels. The divider is tenoned into the side. Note that the bottle tray is upside-down at this stage

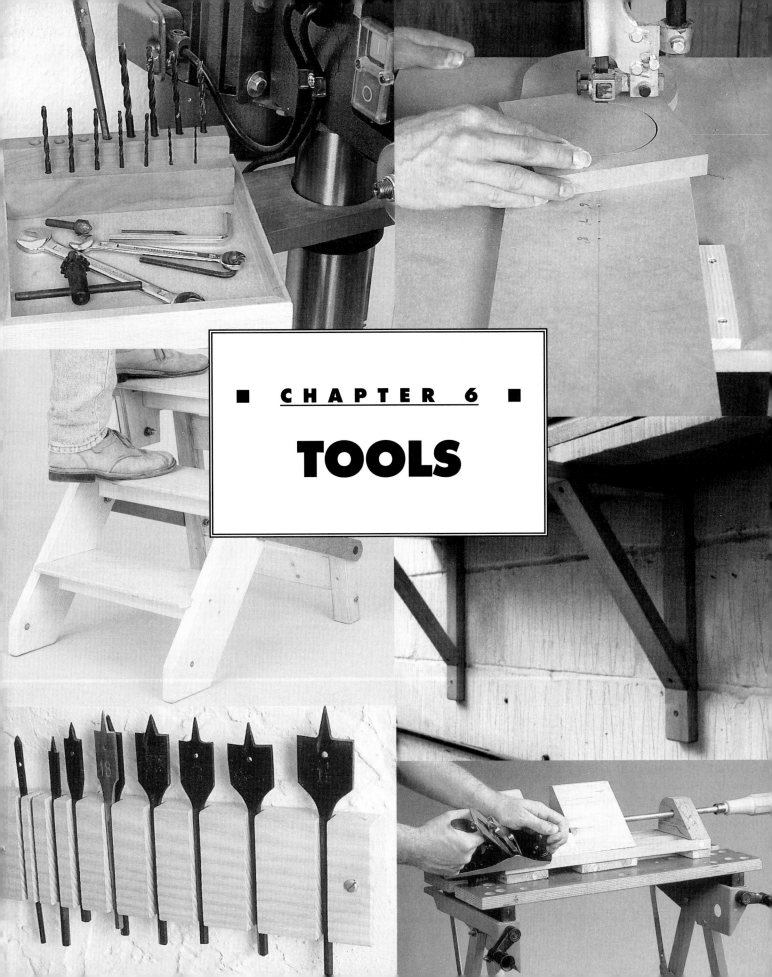

■ CHAPTER 6 ■

TOOLS

A short set of steps is an essential addition to any workshop, especially when it doubles as a work platform. The stringers and rear legs, as supporting parts, are best made from solid timber, but the rest can be of ply or similar. They are quick to assemble with only screws and glue required, and some bolts for the folding action.

HOW TO MAKE A SET OF STEPS

1 Start by marking out a measuring rod on a piece of card or ply. Make it full size showing the joints and the essential angles.

2 Make the rear frame, taking the measurements from the rod. You may only need a rod of the side elevation of the platform, showing the angles, but that should show the positions of the mortices on the uprights, if little else. Tenon the rails into the uprights, or stiles, with through tenons for the greatest strength. If you want to make the steps restorable, hold the mortice and tenon joints in place

Start by making the rear frame using mortice and tenon joints, having, of course, drawn out a measuring rod for marking out the components

The marking out rod is essential and will save you hours of time. It is especially useful whenever you are making a piece that involves angles

Make a card or hardboard template to mark out the curved top of the stringers and the angles at the foot of the steps

Always double - if not triple - check the positions of the step housings against the rod. Remember to make one left-handed and one right-handed string

For the bracket cheeks, first make a template for the angles, having marked out the template with a sliding bevel

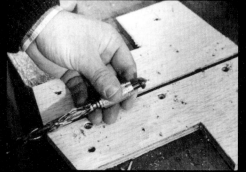

It is when you are countersinking this bracket cheeks that you must remember that one is left-handed and the other is right-handed. It is easy to drill them all on the same side

with a screw near the shoulder.

3 The trick with the stairs is that the steps are all equidistant apart so that as you walk up or down them your steps are consistent. To calculate the gaps measure the length of the stringer, take away the combined thickness of the two steps and divide by three. It is important to account for the gap between the top of the platform and the top of the stringer when you work out how far apart the steps need to be. The treads have a pitch of 55°.

4 Cut the housings for the treads with a router or just with a saw and chisel. Do remember when marking out and cutting the housings that the stringers have to be made in pairs for the right and left!

5 Screw the steps together, with a batten under each tread to carry some weight and improve the triangulation. In this project, 44mm (1¾ in) No. 8 Pozidriv screws were used, which need no pilot hole and tend not to rust.

6 The top assembly governs the folding of the platform. It is made up of two pairs of L-shaped cheeks that sandwich the stringers

and rear uprights. A packing piece screwed to each of the inside cheeks takes account of the difference in thickness of the uprights and stringers.

7 Make a template of the cheeks before cutting them to shape. When drilling the countersunk clearance holes, remember that the cheeks are handed. Screw two battens flat underneath the top, and screw the inside cheeks to them, and the packing pieces to those. Finally fix the outer cheeks in place, and the two supporting joists underneath the top.

8 Place the string between the cheeks and drill for the coachbolts. Do the same for the legs, and with steps assembled, mark the positions for the

retaining cross-piece, which is bolted to the stringer and the leg. Use double washers and locking nuts on the joints that move.

CUTTING LIST

	MATERIAL	QTY	LENGTH	WIDTH	THKNS
A Stringer	Pine	2	640mm	132mm	28mm
B Upright	Pine	2	500mm	45mm	45mm
C Rail	Pine	2	450mm	75mm	19mm
D Cross-piece	Pine	2	370mm	45mm	12mm
E Tread	Ply	2	410mm	195mm	12mm
F Top	Ply	1	505mm	300mm	12mm
G Bracket cheek	Ply	4	270mm	12mm	140mm
H Packing piece	Ply	2	210mm	12mm	140mm
I Cleat	Pine	2	270mm	47mm	19mm
J Step rail	Pine	2	390mm	45mm	19mm
K Top rail	Pine	2	330mm	45mm	19mm

● ● ● ● ●
TOOLS YOU WILL NEED

● PENCIL AND RULE
● HAND SAW
● SET SQUARE
● SLIDING BEVEL
For setting the angles on the stair housings
● BRACE AND BIT OR ELECTRIC DRILL
For boring holes for bolts
● ROUTER
For cutting housings, if you have one. Otherwise use a saw and chisel
● COPING SAW OR JIGSAW
To cut curve on top of stringer
● SCREWDRIVER
● SPANNER
● CHISEL
● COUNTERSINK BIT

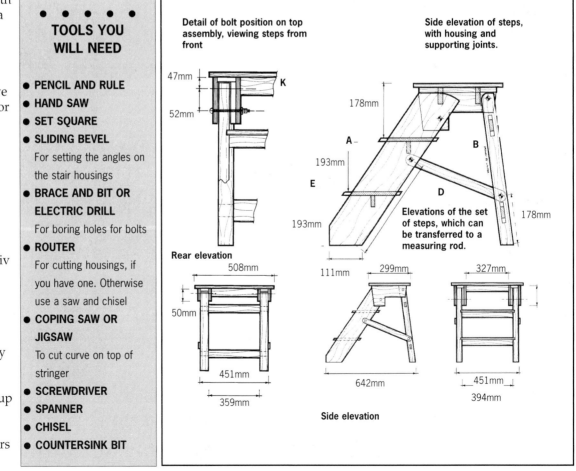

Detail of bolt position on top assembly, viewing steps from front

47mm
52mm
K

Rear elevation

508mm
50mm
451mm
359mm

Side elevation of steps, with housing and supporting joints.

178mm
A
193mm
E
193mm
B
D
178mm

Elevations of the set of steps, which can be transferred to a measuring rod.

111mm   299mm   327mm
642mm
451mm
394mm

Side elevation

115

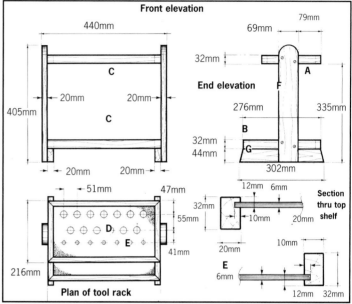

Front elevation

440mm

79mm

69mm

32mm

C

405mm

20mm   20mm

C

End elevation

A

F

276mm   335mm

B

32mm
44mm

G

302mm

20mm   20mm

12mm 6mm

Section thru top shelf

32mm

10mm

20mm

55mm

51mm   47mm

D

E

216mm

41mm

10mm

20mm

E

6mm

12mm 32mm

Plan of tool rack

Keep your most essential tools in order with this set of portable shelves.

HOW TO MAKE THE TOOL RACK

1 Start by making the frame components (A, B and C) for the two shelves. You can use 50x25mm PAR (planed all round) softwood for this, but anything will do. The frames are mitred at the corners, and the shelf is held in a routed groove. If you do not have a router you can screw the shelf to the lower edge of the frame, or even use a solid piece of MDF with no frame. Rout the groove before cutting the parts to length. This saves a lot of time. Rout the groove about 10mm deep for the shelf, then cut the frame parts roughly to length.

2 Using a mitre saw or mitre box, cut the 45° on each of the frame parts. It is important that the four long parts (C) are exactly the same length, but you can adapt the other four parts (A and B) to suit.

3 Cut the two MDF shelves (D and E) to size, making sure there is space for the frame joints to be tightened fully. Drill the top shelf for tools.

4 Cramp up the shelves with a band cramp. Cut out the feet (G) and uprights (F). Screw the uprights to the shelves and the feet to the uprights, without glue for any repair.

CUTTING LIST

	LENGTH	WIDTH	THKNS
A (2off, PAR)	216mm	32mm	20mm
B (2off, PAR)	279mm	32mm	20mm
C (4off, PAR)	400mm	32mm	20mm
D (1off, MDF)	382mm	260mm	6mm
E (1off, MDF)	382mm	260mm	6mm
F (2off, PAR)	405mm	69mm	20mm
G (2off, PAR)	302mm	44mm	20mm

The easiest way to make the shelves is with a router, grooving the frames. You could just pin the base of each shelf to the under edge of the frame, or use solid MDF

Cut mitres on the end of each frame component and then assemble, using a band clamp, with the pre-drilled base inside. Vary the holes to suit your tools

Drill clearance holes in the uprights and then screw them to the frames of the shelves. Do not glue them as you may want to adjust or repair them in the future

A foolproof way to cut circles of almost any size on a bandsaw. The idea of this project is that you attach the workpiece to a swing arm, which you can move into the blade. Then you can start spinning the wood to form a circle.

HOW TO MAKE THE BANDSAW JIG

1 The first step is to make yourself a base. Fix battens to the underside of the base, so that you can position the base each time without fuss. Any odd bits of softwood will do for the battens, and MDF is probably best for the base as it is very even, smooth and stable. Perfect for jigs.

2 Line up locating holes, checking that the pivot point and the blade are in line. Mark out the locating holes and the pivot point on the swing arm. Note that the radius is determined by the distance from the blade to the locating holes. Fix the arm to the base and cut a straight line, to hit the line on which you have marked the locating holes and the pivot point. Measure along the line to show the intervals for the locating holes. These can be to any distance, depending on the work in hand. Drill the obvious holes at the standard distances, 1in, 2in and so on. Also drill the pivot point. Now cut the curved section at the end of the arm and screw the arm to the base.

3 Fix the base to the bandsaw table, with the battens against the sides of the table, and bring the arm up against the blade. Now screw a stop to the base so that the arm cannot go any further. In use, you start spinning when the arm hits this stop.

4 Screw a piece of wood (any shape) to the arm. Now screw the arm back onto the base, and away you go. Turn on the bandsaw and push the arm against the stop. Start spinning the wood and you'll soon have a perfect circle.

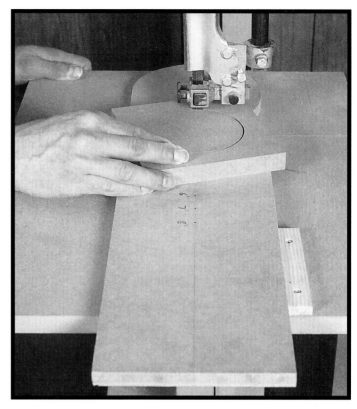

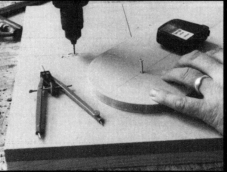

Plan view of the circle cutting jig

173mm (6¹³/₁₆")
77mm (3¹/₃₂")
LOCATION HOLES
25mm (1") INTERVALS
586mm (23¹/₁₆")

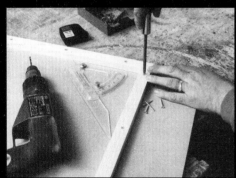

First fix battens to the bottom of the base board. These position the base on the bandsaw table

Draw a line on the arm for the locating holes and the pivot point. Drill the pivot hole and screw to the base

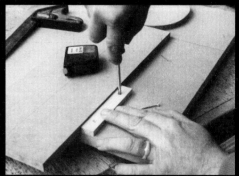

Now fix the stop to the base so that when you push in the arm it can go no further

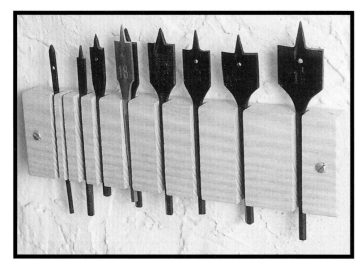

This flatbit rack is one simple step towards keeping your workshop tidy.

HOW TO MAKE THE RACK

1 First select and prepare a piece of ash, or a hardwood that is as tough. Plane the sides and edges, and check that everything is perfectly square.

2 Square a line across one end, 6mm (1/4 in), and mark out the grooves (according to the plan) with a try square and pencil or ballpoint pen. Extend the lines, using a try square resting against the edges and a gauge set to the depth of the grooves.

3 To work by hand, use a tenon saw and bench hook to cut each groove, taking care to cut against the line on the waste side.

4 Use a 6mm (1/4 in) chisel and a mallet to chip away the waste wood carefully from one end of each groove. Work from a groove in the middle of the wood first, to avoid splitting the grain on the narrowest grooves. Cut the shoulders of the grooves and in between to make chiselling easier.

5 Reverse the wood and remove waste from the other side. Do not break through the ends. Clean up the bottom of the groove by paring with the chisel.

6 A quicker method is to use a radial arm saw, adjusting the blade height and working to the lines.

This lets you fine tune the width of grooves, especially ones for smaller flatbits that are friction held.

7 Mark out, drill and countersink holes for attaching the rack to your workshop wall. Carefully cut off the ends to the line, using a tenon saw.

8 Use a plane to remove saw burrs and to bevel the edges, then an abrasive paper block to finally clean up. Be careful not to snap off any of the short grain between the grooves.

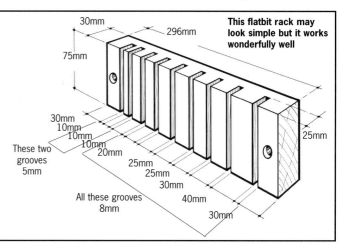

This flatbit rack may look simple but it works wonderfully well

30mm
296mm
75mm
30mm
10mm
10mm
10mm
These two grooves 5mm
20mm
25mm
25mm
25mm
30mm
All these grooves 8mm
40mm
30mm
25mm

Use a gauge to mark the depth of the grooves. You will be able to plane away this marking line later

The radial arm saw makes quick work of the grooves. Do not hold the rack by the short end when cutting

The advantage of a radial arm saw is that it can be used for snipping off the shavings for a better fit

An adaptable, sturdy and self-standing rolling support to assist your sawing work.

HOW TO MAKE THE ROLLER STAND

1 Cut out all the parts, chamfering the edges and removing any rough corners. The base does not have to be a single plate, if you prefer legs or a tripod of sorts.

2 Mark a cross on the underneath of the base and drill and countersink holes to attach the cross members on top. One rail is screwed to the base on edge - to which the upright is fixed - and the other face down.

3 Having fixed the rails, insert a screw into each end of the dowel or broom handle, then cut off the head and prepare the uprights into which the roller will fit.

4 Cut the main upright to length. This needs to be slotted so that it can be retained by a bolt. Mark out the slot, drilling at each end as access for a coping saw or jigsaw. A plunging router would be quickest for cutting the slot, using a fence.

5 The top rail assembly is screwed and glued to the slotted upright. The short uprights for the roller form the ends of the top rail, fixed on plywood cheeks. The main upright is screwed and glued between the ply cheeks. If the upright is not

the same thickness as the ends, you will need to pad it out to fit properly between the cheeks. Screw one end to one cheek, and then fix that to the upright, with packing pieces if required. Insert the roller, and screw the other end and cheek in place.

6 Now you can start building the box in which the main upright moves. Take one face of the plywood box and pin the two narrow edges to it. Remember to make the edges that bit longer than the faces by th thickness of the cross-piece on the base, on which the upright sits.

7 Once the glue has dried, you can screw the partly assembled box to the cross-piece on the base, from the inside. That way the sawheads are hidden inside the box. Then the other box face can be pinned in place.

8 Mark the point on the box faces for the bolt hole. Find the position for the hole by resting the upright next to the box, in its lowest position and

marking a line across. The hole should be central to the face of the box and upright. Fit the upright in the box, locate the bolt, with a wingnut at one end, and adjust for use. The wonderful thing about a roller support is that it can be adjusted to the height of any machinery - or even a workbench - in the workshop.

Elevations and plan of roller stand

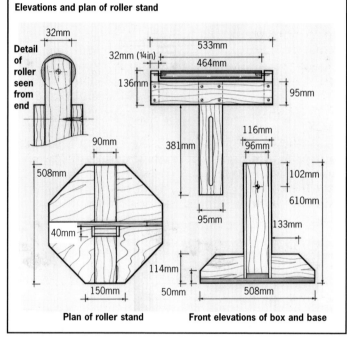

Detail of roller seen from end

32mm

32mm (¼in)

533mm

464mm

136mm

95mm

90mm

116mm

96mm

508mm

381mm

102mm

610mm

40mm

95mm

133mm

114mm

150mm

50mm

508mm

Plan of roller stand **Front elevations of box and base**

Cut up the parts for the base, upright and base rails. Any old offcut will do, but the more consistent the thickness and width the better

Shape and chamfer the vertical base rail and cut out a notch, then screw it from underneath. This holds the box assembly

Build the box around the upright, using glue and 25mm (1in) panel pins. Only assemble three sides so the box can be fixed to the base

CUTTING LIST

	LENGTH	WIDTH	THKNS
A Top (1)	848mm	70mm	44mm
B Leg (4)	510mm	70mm	44mm
C Brace (2)	205mm	205mm	10mm

How to make a sawhorse with a standard splay for ease.

HOW TO MAKE THE SAWHORSE

1 The thing to note about this sawhorse is that the legs splay out at the same angle in both dimensions. That means you can mark out the cutting with one setting of 105° on your sliding bevel. To make it easier, the lengthwise splay is made by angling the housing joint in the top (A), and the lateral splay by planing a bevel on the top of each leg (B). Start by cutting the top and legs to length.

2 Mark out the housings on the top. Do not be fooled that the housing is angled in two dimensions. It is in fact flat bottomed. Angling the depth of a housing is a bit awkward. Cut the shoulders of the housing with a tenon saw, and then chisel out the waste. Pare from both sides to reduce the risk of breakout.

3 Now you can cut the angled halving joint on the end of each leg. Mark around the leg with the sliding bevel for the shoulder, and then mark the angle down from the top. Cut the shoulder and then cut the face of the joint.

4 Drill and countersink the legs to fix to the top. Glue and screw them in place and then offer up a piece of MDF, ply or chipboard as a brace, and mark out its shape. Drill the brace for fixing screws and attach it to the legs. You can also add a wider replaceable top.

Start by cutting the housings in the top of the sawhorse. This house is flat bottomed, not angled. The splay is cut from the top of each leg

Using the same setting on your sliding bevel as for the housings, mark out and cut the angled halving joint on the top of each leg. Shade the waste

For reinforcement add a brace to the legs to support the housing joint. Offer up a piece of MDF, mark on the shape, drill and countersink, and then fix

---

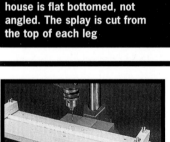

CUTTING LIST

	LENGTH	WIDTH	THKNS
A Clamp (2)	90mm	23mm	28mm
B V-piece (1)	476mm	45mm	27mm
C Base (14)	476mm	90mm	20mm

Make a jig for repetitive drilling of round wood.

HOW TO MAKE THE DRILLING JIG

1 The principle of the jig is that it has a V-groove in which the dowel sits. The V must not be too deep, but must be wide enough to take the most common diameters of dowel. The easiest way is to make the V is to bevel two pieces and then join them together. Start by bevelling those parts, and then screw them to a base piece.

2 Drill through the base and V-pieces for bolts to hole the two clamping pieces. Cut a V in each of the clamps (A) and drill them for the bolt. In use, tighten the wing-nuts to hold dowel.

Start by planing up the two V-pieces (B). Mark up the bevel with a marking gauge and then plane it all off or remove same waste on a bandsaw first

Screw the V-pieces to the base board (C). The V must not be too deep or the dowel will be lost. Equally it needs to be able to take dowel of most diameters

Cut a V from each clamping piece (A) then hold it to the rest of the jig for drilling the holes for the bolts. Counterbore underneath the base for the heads

These gallows brackets provide excellent timber storage, and are an ideal introduction to dovetail joints.

HOW TO MAKE THE BRACKETS

1 Square a line round the end of the top and upright, 27mm (1¹⁄₁₆ in) from the end. This size is 2mm (³⁄₃₂ in) greater than the thickness of the wood to allow for the excess to be planed off after you have assembled the joint.

2 Mark and cut out the dovetail joints, doing the tail on the top piece first. Make it 36mm (1¹³⁄₃₂ in) wide at the end and 25mm (1in) at the shoulder to give you a slope of 1:6. Then mark out the pins.

3 Make sure that the joints fit well, and drill the holes for the fixings; put one close to the top and the second below the strut. Cut the top and upright to length, and chamfer the outer ends to improve the look and reduce the risk of snagging.

4 Cut the strut to length and use a marking gauge to mark a line across each end, at half the thickness, for the bevel. With the bracket laid on its side, position the strut on top and mark on it the points at which its back face cuts across the bracket.

This shows the length of bevel required, which can now be cut.

Offer up the strut again and mark the notches to be cut from the bracket, with the dovetail apart.

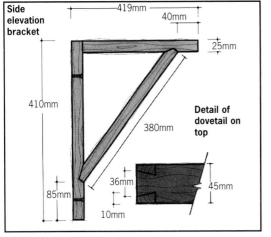

Side elevation bracket

419mm
40mm
25mm
410mm
380mm
Detail of dovetail on top
36mm
45mm
85mm
10mm

GLUING UP

Hold the dovetail with a sash cramp when gluing, using a packing piece narrower than the tail to pull the pieces together. Make sure that the bracket is square by adjusting the cramp head in or out until the parts are exactly at right angles to each other. If you don't have a sash cramp, simply use a woodscrew to hold the parts together, countersinking the head well below the surface. When the glue has set, plane off the protruding ends of the joints.

The strut is fixed by holding the assembled parts together in the vice, and drilling holes for the No. 8 screws. These go in at right angles to the struts, so that they grip as much wood as possible. Screw the brackets to the wall before you glue the struts on. Clean with abrasive paper, and finish with paint or polyurethane.

Cut the tails first. Take the two pieces of timber to be joined. Add 1mm to the thickness of the timber, to give excess to the joint (as above) and measure that distance in from the end of each piece. Square a line on this mark all the way round the wood for the shoulder

Use the tail to mark out the pins on the end-grain of the outer piece, held in a vice. Then use a try square (or the parallel part of a dovetail template) to mark lines downwards from these markings, on both faces. Make a cut line across the bottom of the pin with a marking knife

Cutting the pins accurately is the critical part of a tight-fitting joint. Most people are too cautious. Saw down on the waste side of the line, leaving just the line and no more.
If you saw into the waste you will need a chisel to make the joint fit. Then cut out most of waste with a coping saw

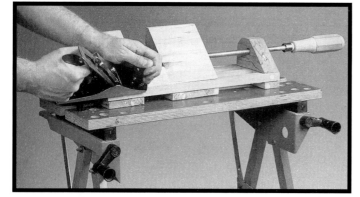

CUTTING LIST

	MATERIAL	QTY	LENGTH	WIDTH	THKNS
A Vice rail	Beech	1	450mm	50mm	30mm
B Plane rest	Beech	1	450mm	45mm	30mm
C Planing block	Beech	1	215mm	110mm	50mm
D Planing block	Beech	1	215mm	80mm	50mm
E Planing block	Beech	1	215mm	50mm	25mm
F Slide rail	Beech	5	450mm	25mm	20mm
G Block retainer	Beech	1	125mm	110mm	15mm
H Block retainer	Beech	1	110mm	90mm	15mm
J Block retainer	Beech	1	110mm	45mm	15mm
K Tailstock	Beech	1	125mm	70mm	45mm
L Handle	Beech	1	180mm	40mm	40mm

This tool allows you to shoot mitres and right-angled end-grain accurately and quickly.

HOW TO MAKE THE BLOCK

1 Glue up the planing blocks but do not cut them into two pieces yet. Make sure the heart sides oppose each other before you glue them.

2 Cut the 45° angle. You can cut the angle on a bandsaw, or use a ripsaw, leaving the cut slightly proud and planing to finish.

Check the angle with a sliding bevel.

3 Cut the rails, spacers, slides, vice rail and tailstock to size. Drill holes into the rails and fence and countersink them.

4 Glue the rails together, placing the spacers between them.

When set, drill and counterbore and insert 50mm (2in) No. 12 screws, from both sides. Plug the holes, and if you don't have a plug cutter, take the wood to be used for the plug and drill a shallow hole with the bit you used for the counterbore as a guide. Roughly cut out the plug, then pare around the edge of the hole to make it slightly cone shaped.

5 Bury a nut in the tailstock. Shape the tailstock and drill the screw-thread hole oversize. Cut the tailstock in half along the hole. Measure the dimensions of the nut and mark out a recess for it across the drill hole, two-thirds of the way along the hole from the handle end. Chisel out a slot to fit half the nut, and make a corresponding slot in the other half. The nut must fit as tightly as possible. Bed in epoxy adhesive and glue the two parts together. Screw the tailstock to the rails. Use a square to keep it true.

TOOLS YOU WILL NEED

- HANDSAW OR BANDSAW
- DRILL
- SLIDING BEVEL
- LATHE

MATERIALS YOU WILL NEED

- BEECH
  1130x110x50mm
  Or softwood - face the shooting surfaces with hardwood
- COPPER PIPE
- THREADED BAR
- WASHERS to fit bar
- 2 X NUTS, to fit bar
- SCREWS

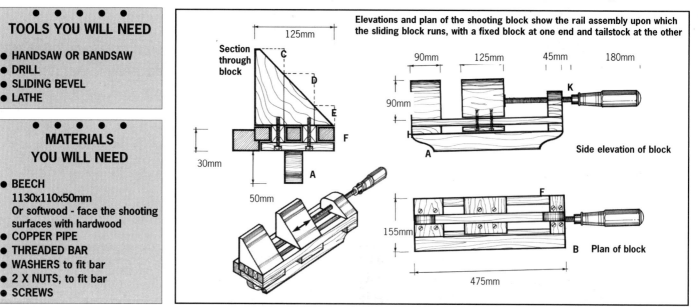

Elevations and plan of the shooting block show the rail assembly upon which the sliding block runs, with a fixed block at one end and tailstock at the other

Section through block

125mm

30mm

50mm

Side elevation of block

Plan of block

90mm   125mm   45mm   180mm

90mm

155mm

475mm

6 Mark out the end block and the sliding block, and screw the end block part to the sliding spacer. Check everything with a square. Saw the blocks apart, using a deep, fine tenon saw or a fine-toothed panel saw.

7 Hold the sliding block against the tailstock and mark the hole centre for the threaded bar. Drill a hole 3mm (⅛in) deep, the size of a 45mm (125⁄32in) washer, then drill another 3mm (⅛in) deep hole inside the first hole to take a 13mm (½in) washer.

8 Weld or glue (with epoxy resin) a 13mm (½in) washer to the end of the threaded bar, by positioning the nut near the end of the bar, sitting the washer on top and fixing the washer in position. This washer is sunk in the shallow recess you have drilled in the sliding block. To pull the sliding block you need to fix a 45mm (125⁄32in) washer over the recess on the block.

Drill three holes in the washer to take No. 6 roundhead screws. Taper the end of the bar for 25mm (1in) using a bench grinder, to fit into the handle.

9 Thread the bar into the tailstock, and fit the sliding block onto the bar with the large washer, making sure the 13mm (½in) washer is moving freely. Screw the slides into place under the block and adjust the tightness of the screws on the sliding block so that the block slides smoothly.

10 Cut and shape the vice bar, and screw in place on the bottom of the rail assembly. Cut and rebate the plane rest, which runs along the rails, and fit onto the upright side of blocks. The plane rest needs to be below the top edge of the rails - the distance between the side of your plane and the blade is about right.

11 Turn or shape the handle, and tap home the ferrule, protecting it with scrap, before drilling out the centre with a 12.5mm (½in) bit to save it from splitting. Put some epoxy glue in the hole and thread the handle home, wrapping some rag around the bar and holding it with a pair of Mole grips. Rub in several coats of linseed oil.

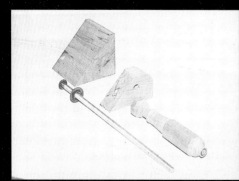
Laminate up the blocks from planks, with the grain direction alternating to ensure stability is maintained

Cramp up the rail and spacer assembly having cut the block to 45° on a bandsaw or with a handsaw

It is easiest to do most of the work on the blocks as one piece and then cut in two with a handsaw or tenon saw

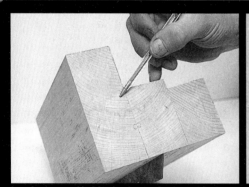
The sliding block is attached to the handle via a captive nut in the tailstock and washers in the block

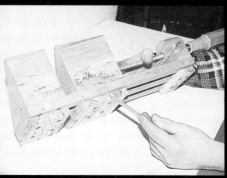
Screw the sliding plate underneath the rails to the sliding block, so that the block slides smoothly

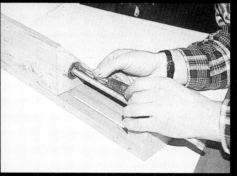
Screw the large washer to the sliding block so that the washer welded to the end of the bar pulls on it

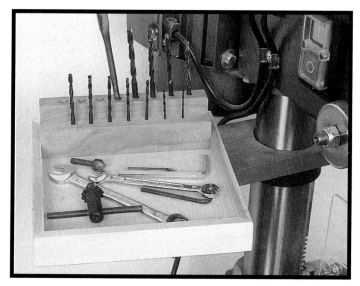

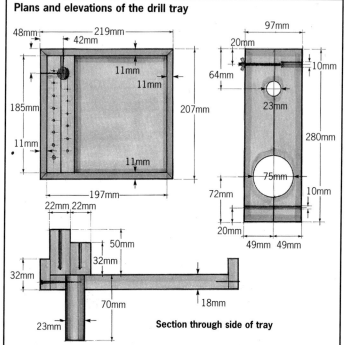

Plans and elevations of the drill tray

Keep drill bits and chuck keys tidy with this pillar drill tray.

HOW TO MAKE THE DRILL TRAY

1 Start by getting the collar right. This fits around the column. The collar has a hole for the column and a hole for the piece of dowel that joins the tray to the collar. Draw a centre line along the board for the collar. Drill a hole for the dowel.

If you have a holesaw, drill out the hole for the column. An alternative method is to mark out the hole with a compass at this stage and cut the board in half, before you make the hole for the column. Before anything else, drill the two bolt holes across the width of the collar near each end. Depending on the length of the bolts you can find, counterbore the hole from one side. Now you are pretty much ready to cut the collar in half.

2 Use a bandsaw or jigsaw to cut the column hole roughly to size and then clean up with a drum sander. You are now about ready to make the drill tray.

3 Take a piece of MDF or ply to check what size you want the tray to be. This depends upon your pillar drill. Fit the collar to the column and rest an offcut on it to check the size. Cut the base to size. Drill the bottom of the base to take the dowel for the collar, but do not glue it in place quite yet.

4 Prepare the sides of the tray. These are pinned and glued to the base, with mitre joints at the ends. Once those have set fit the two blocks for the drill bits. Drill these for your most popular bits, making sure you do not forget countersinks and other odds and ends for drilling.

5 Glue the dowel into the base of the tray, and glue the bit blocks into the top of the tray. It is now ready to fit to the drill.

6 You need to take the collar apart to fit around the column.

CUTTING LIST			
	LENGTH	WIDTH	THKNS
A Collar (1)	280mm	97mm	22mm
B Dowel (1)	70mm	23mm	23mm
C Base (1)	197mm	185mm	18mm
D Side (2)	219mm	32mm	11mm
E End (2)	207mm	32mm	11mm

Drill the hole for the dowel before you split the collar in two. The drill will wander otherwise

Drill the two blocks for your bits. Make sure the holes are spaced widely enough for easy access

If possible, find wingnuts for the bolts. That way you can adjust the tray if it gets in the way

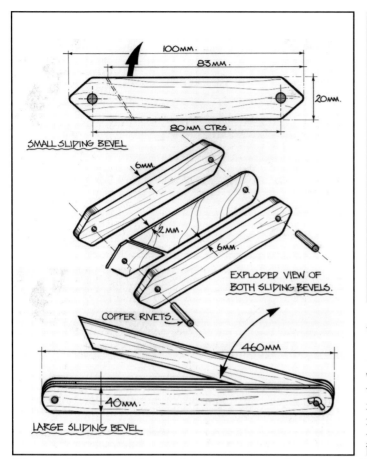

SMALL SLIDING BEVEL

100MM.

83MM.

20MM

80MM CTRS.

6MM

2MM.

6MM.

EXPLODED VIEW OF
BOTH SLIDING BEVELS.

COPPER RIVETS.

460MM

40MM.

LARGE SLIDING BEVEL

Discover how to use rivets to make your own sliding bevel from wood or brass for marking out angles on jobs of any size.

HOW TO MAKE A BRASS BEVEL

1 Clamp the brass for the blade and two faces in a vice to file both sides flat and parallel. Mark them to drill a hole at each end for a rivet. Use copper rod for the rivets, cut slightly long so that they will be slightly proud. Mark the holes for the rivets with a centre punch, and drill for a snug fit for the copper rod.

2 Cut the blade at an angle to produce the spacer at one end.

Push the copper rod through the hole, and lightly tap the rivet with the ball side of a ball-pein hammer to turn over the head.

3 Alternate between the two ends of the rivet, until the face pieces are held firmly but the blade can move freely. It might help to put a piece of paper between the faces and the blade, until the riveting is done to ensure you do not rivet too tightly. Nor must it be too loose for holding at an angle. For a simpler gauge you could just rivet two lengths of brass strip together. Use a copper nail and washer to do this.

4 For a larger gauge, metal is not suitable. Instead of brass you could use three strips of ash, and a roofing bolt and wingnut in place of the rivet. Glue up the fixed end of the stock, using a spacer again, and resting the bevel on glass for clamping gluing and screwing.

When you put the brass sliding bevel together you will need to have the rivets overlong. You can turn one end of each rivet over and then work on the other side

Use the ball end of a pein hammer to round over the rivet. Insert a piece of paper between the faces and the blade temporarily so as not to rivet too tightly

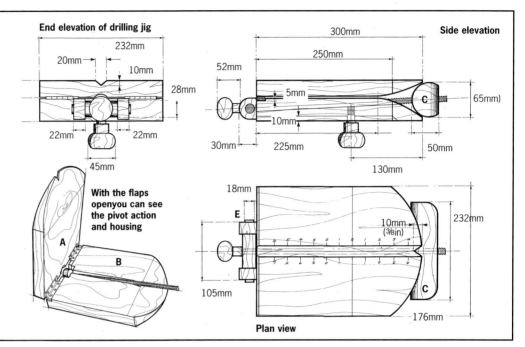

End elevation of drilling jig

232mm
20mm
10mm
28mm
22mm
22mm
45mm

With the flaps open you can see the pivot action and housing

A
B

Side elevation

300mm
250mm
52mm
5mm
65mm)
10mm
30mm
225mm
50mm
130mm

Plan view

18mm
E
10mm (⅜in)
232mm
105mm
C
176mm

The jig consists of two flaps (A and B). These are hinged to one another so that they can open, or lie flat. A wedge (C) opens the flaps. Through the wedge runs a screw thread (D). By turning the screw the wedge is pulled towards the hinge, so raising the top flap (A). The lower flap (B) is bolted or cramped to the table of your pillar drill. The important thing is that the screw thread must itself pivot so that it rises as the wedge approaches the hinge.

To accommodate the pivoting thread, groove the lower flap so that the two flaps can lie flat.

HOW TO MAKE THE DRILLING JIG

1 Cut out the flap pieces (A and B). Make sure the grain is running along their length. Work on the pivoting action before shaping the flaps for the wedge. Then cut out the two pivot arms (E) and shape a short stub tenon on each. Cut two corresponding mortices in the lower flap.

Drill the arms for the pivot (F), having drilled the pivot for the threaded rod.

2 If you are using wooden threaded rod then cut a length of it now (D). You'll find that ½ in thread will do. If you do not have thread cutting equipment, then use metal studding. In that case you will have to sink a nut into the wedge and glue the knob on the outer end of the studding for adjusting the jig.

3 Cut out the stock for the wedge. Shape the wedge and the opening parts of the flaps. Cut a recess along the top back edge of the lower flap for the hinges, and cut a V-groove along the main axis of the top flap. Then turn the spacer (G), which stops the wedge and threaded rod being pulled out.

4 Assemble the pivot arms with the pivot in place, and then hinge the two flaps together. Glue the knob to the end of the rod and feed the rod through the pivot, gluing the spacer in place. Add a bolt underneath, for fixing the jig to the table.

The chain is designed to stop the top flap flipping over and breaking the hinges. Feed the thread into the wedge and then mark where the wedge needs to be for the most common angles you drill.

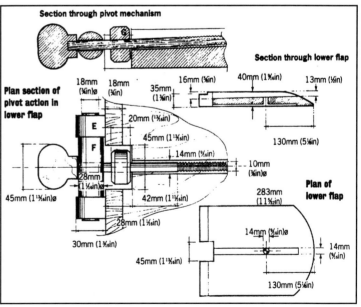

Section through pivot mechanism

G

Section through lower flap

16mm (⅝in)
40mm (1⅝in)
13mm (½in)
130mm (5⅛in)

Plan section of pivot action in lower flap

18mm (¾in)ø
18mm (¾in)
35mm (1⅜in)
20mm (1¾in)
45mm (1¾in)
14mm (⅝in)
10mm (⅜in)ø
E
F
28mm (1⅛in)
42mm (1¾in)
45mm (1¹³⁄₁₆in)ø
28mm (1⅛in)
30mm (1⅛in)
45mm (1¹³⁄₁₆in)

Plan of lower flap

283mm (11½in)
14mm (⅝in)ø
14mm (⅝in)
130mm (5⅛in)